Birth of the
JERSEY SHORE

The Personalities & Politics that
Built America's Resort

RANDALL GABRIELAN

THE
History
PRESS

Published by The History Press
Charleston, SC 29403
www.historypress.net

Front cover, top left: The high-rise, begun in 1973, was abandoned unfinished after the builder's 1974 bankruptcy. For years known as "the skeleton," the project, which endured, as does the Jersey Shore, was completed in 1982. Named the Admiralty, the condominiumized building overlooks the water in Monmouth Beach. *Author's photo.*

Cover background images courtesy of the Library of Congress.

First published 2015

Manufactured in the United States

ISBN 978.1.62619.706.0

Library of Congress Control Number: 2015932932

Notice: The information in this book is true and complete to the best of our knowledge. It is offered without guarantee on the part of the author or The History Press. The author and The History Press disclaim all liability in connection with the use of this book.

CONTENTS

CONTENTS

CONTENTS

CONTENTS

ACKNOWLEDGEMENTS

I thank the many who contributed, notably three facilities in Ocean County. Special merit to the Ocean County Historical Society, their librarian Betsy Dudas and her volunteers; the Ocean County Cultural and Heritage Commission and Division Director Timothy G. Hart; and the New Jersey Maritime Museum and curator Deborah Whitcraft. Lenders of pictures are acknowledged under their contributions. Unacknowledged pictures are mine.

I thank all who provided information. Special appreciation goes to professionals who contributed from their own work, including Joan Berkey, architectural historian, and Margaret Westfield, preservation architect. Thanks to Gerald Beer, Margaret Buchholz, Patricia H. Burke, Eileen Chapman, Judith Courter, Elaine and Roy Everett, Susan Sandlass Gardiner, Kathleen Heim, Bob Hentges, Ferd Klebold, Gil Leibrick, G.W.C. "Bill" McCarter, Casey Madrick of United States Military Academy Archives, Don Nyce, Gary Saretzky and Pete Stemmer.

INTRODUCTION

My narrative history of the Jersey Shore will reveal early explorers, our once-unoccupied beaches with the subsistence living of nearby residents, dangerous maritime trades, the spreading of splendid resorts and the shore's transformation to a residential domain. These crucial topics may render a risk of omitting the people who shaped the shore. Human interest adds color and life to inanimate structures and environments, so those who made the shore New Jersey's most endearing landscape merit their own volume.

This work had numerous choices for inclusion, but space constraints influenced selection and length of the biographical sketches. The book includes many of the shore's most important figures, but subjectivity influenced the selection of interesting figures who added color and depth to the shore's past. Some were picked to the exclusion of others with greater significance. Others have stories that merit elevation from historical obscurity. Selection was an art of balancing significance, interest and merit. This is purview of the author, and not only do I take responsibility for the biographical lineup, but I will match this group of 114 entries against any other of that number for any standard of measure.

The organization is first topical, then alphabetical. Birth and death dates are enumerated when known. Thus, the table of contents will direct the reader to fields of interest, while subjects' dates will provide insight to any period.

A variety of checked sources were utilized for most entries. In some instance sources are specified in the profiles while others are noted in the selected bibliography. No attempt was made to cite well-known information.

ARTISTS AND ARCHITECTS

Ernest A. Arend (1876-1950)

Ernest Augustus Arend, born in Trenton, represents skilled local architects with scant biographical records but in possession of large bodies of fine work. They should be known by their commissions, notably Arend, a major Monmouth figure of the first third of the twentieth century.

Arend initially practiced in his native city in the Brouse and Arend firm. He relocated to Asbury Park around 1900, leaving the Trenton office to former partner Samuel Brouse. Arend's career was centered in the environs of Asbury Park and the Red Bank area where he lived. One of his earliest buildings is the North Asbury Park Engine and Hose Company, a frame, extant Classical Revival structure. He secured numerous municipal and school contracts. These included Asbury Park High School and Stadium from the late 1920s. Earlier he designed there what was the latest advance in segregated education, the 1913 Bangs Avenue School, now the closed Barack Obama School, two separate buildings, the larger for whites and the smaller for blacks, each with entrances on adjoining streets, the two connected by an auditorium for mutual use.

In Middletown, by 1920, he had expanded the Leonardo High School, which had been completed only a few years prior, and the modest Port Monmouth School. This simple Colonial Revival design was reinterpreted with greater flourish ten years later with the Leonardo Elementary School. Perhaps Arend's most visible school project is the former Neptune High School located on the east side of Highway 71 or Main Street, a short

Ernest Arend's design "Blossom Cove" became the site that mandated equalized valuation.

distance south of Asbury Park, a building now adaptively used as the Jersey Shore Arts Center. Other large prominent Monmouth school projects include the 1928 Collegiate Gothic former Long Branch High School and the 1917 Red Bank High School, now a middle school.

Arend utilized the Colonial Revival as one of his two favored residential designs, including 2 Blossom Cove Road, Middletown. At number 44 is his other style, the Italian Renaissance Revival for Everett Brown. This house became a center of the United States croquet sport when owned by Olivia Switz. It also became a real estate landmark as her successful appeal of an assessment, the case *Switz v. Middletown*, established the principle of equalized valuation. Arend regularly utilized this stucco-clad model, modified for houses of varied sizes, including his own built on upper Broad Street, Red Bank, one since destroyed. This design also appeared as a sample house of the National Fireproofing Company (NATCO) and in an advertisement for Atlas Portland Cement. Arend was Monmouth County consultant to Sears for mail-order houses.

Arend maintained a New York office, or address, as did many suburban architects. His only known New York City building was a restaurant-loft at 17 West 17th Street, done for an Allenhurst, New Jersey owner. The diversity of his output is further reflected by a 1929 project, a clubhouse built over the water for the Shrewsbury River Yacht Club in Fair Haven.

Arend's affiliations included the Masons, Elks, Asbury Park Rotary and the Monmouth County Society of Architects, forerunner of the Jersey Shore Chapter of the American Institute of Architects. Arend was a key practitioner of his era, with significant commissions that enrich the landscape.

THEODORE R. DAVIS (1840–1894)

Davis, born in Boston, attained great fame as a military artist during the Civil War. He traveled the South and West after the war prior to settling in Asbury Park. Much of Davis's work there awaits rediscovery.

Davis apparently studied under Henry W. Herrick, once a famous engraver but now obscure. After he became a Civil War correspondent and artist for *Harper's Weekly*, Davis experienced extensive action with a number of notable generals. In 1863, while with General James McPherson's corps in Grant's army, Davis was wounded in Mississippi at the Battle of Raymond. He deflected the impression that combat artists had a safe role by claiming that he had a sketch pad shot out of his hands. Davis was also with General William T. Sherman during his Georgia march to the sea.

In the postwar period, Davis was with General George Custer for a spell and spent time in Colorado around mining areas and on buffalo hunts, where he killed as well as drew. His enduring work of the time was the design of the President Rutherford B. Hayes White House china service, a commission he reportedly received after suggesting at a chance encounter with Lucy Hayes that her husband's set should be based on North American flora and fauna. The pieces are among the more desirable of White House collectable dishes.

Davis, who came to Asbury Park around 1880, was befriended by founder James A. Bradley, who set him up with a studio adjacent to the boardwalk. He entertained visitors with tales of his colorful career but surely produced art there. However, little appears able to be traced back to him.

BRIAN P. HANLON (B. 1961)

Brian Hanlon, long known as "New Jersey's Sculptor," now has a national reputation as approximately four hundred of his works stand in fourteen states.

Hanlon was born in Jersey City and moved to Hazlet at age one. He was first inspired by sculpture through a Holmdel High School teacher. However, it was at Monmouth College (now University) where touching the clay made him realize that art could be a life's work. His first public piece was a memorial at Holmdel High to Bob Roggy, a track and field athlete (as was Hanlon), who was tragically killed in an accident. School also inspired his second project, *The Involved Student* at Monmouth, a celebration of the student-athlete, modeled by the star soccer player Michelle

Adamkowski. As Hanlon did graduate work at Boston University, he realized that commissioned art would be the key to sculpture as a career.

Hanlon's first commissioned work was a statue of a praying St. Francis, ordered by the Reverend James Clark for St. Leo the Great Catholic Church, Lincroft. The statue was completed in 1991, the year the sculptor was married. St. Francis's kneeling position was a nod to Brian's proposal to his wife, Michelle, his "Involved Student." Michelle later modeled for Mary, the mother of God. St. Francis was nearly contemporary with Our Lady of Consolation at St. Gabriel's, Marlboro. Hanlon has noted that "the Catholic Church has been the greatest patron of artists in the history of man." He has installed many pieces in the large, great 1992 St. Joseph's in Toms River, the town where his studio is located, and in churches over a wide area.

Athletics has emerged as a major part of Hanlon's output. One early work is a bust of Dwight Stephenson at the Pro Football Hall of Fame in Canton, Ohio. Hanlon is the official sculptor of the Naismith Memorial Basketball Hall of Fame in Springfield, Massachusetts. His sculptures, often larger than life-size, embody the spirit and motion of the players. First responders, notably firefighters, are also regular subjects for Hanlon's work.

Brian Hanlon's *Welcome to Ocean County* celebrates the spirit of the county's residents exemplified after the ravages of Hurricane Sandy.

Hanlon indicated that the Jersey Shore has had a profound impact on him and his outlook on the world. The people he grew up around were inspirational and interesting, in many cases more so than the sculpture itself. Shore subjects include the Fishermen's Memorial at the Manasquan Inlet in Loughran Point, Point Pleasant Beach, installed in 2000 to memorialize the January 1999 loss of two fishing boats from town, each with four fatalities. A second honors the fishing community at the Barnegat Light section of Long Beach Island, while a 2014 bas-relief at the New Jersey Maritime Museum is a tribute to the commercial fishing industry.

Hanlon chose to be illustrated by a 2014 piece that embodies life at the shore and the family as society's fundamental unit. His *Welcome to Ocean County*, a gift to the county from the Jay and Linda Grunin Foundation, recognizes the spirit shown by Ocean's residents in response to the ravages of the 2012 Hurricane Sandy. The scallop shell behind the family group is a tribute to the fishing industry, while the Ferris wheel at the rear of the shell is a nod to the shorefront amusement section at the easternmost end of Highway 37, where the installation stands near Main Street, Toms River.

Hanlon figures, both numerous and varied, include Governor Richard J. Hughes in New Brunswick, Count Basie in Red Bank and *Angel in Anguish*, a passionate September 11 memorial at Windward Beach Park in Brick. Be mindful of the pleasure of unexpectedly spotting a previously unseen Hanlon as I had on the Ocean County Jersey Shore while researching this book.

GERARD RUTGERS HARDENBERGH (1855–1915)

Hardenbergh is compelling as a true Jersey Shore artist as so much of his work reflects his Bay Head environs. His oeuvre also depicts an early interest in ornithology.

Hardenbergh, born in New Brunswick, was the great-great-grandson of Jacob Rutsen Hardenbergh, the first president of Rutgers University and the namesake of Captain Henry Rutgers, for whom Queens College was renamed. He may have been self-taught, as there appear to be no records of study at the Pennsylvania Academy of Fine Arts where he exhibited in the 1880s. Jerry, as he was known, located at Ortley Beach in the early 1890s, prior to his move to Bay Head, where he lived and worked on his houseboat, the *Pelican*. The vessel, moored on Scow Ditch near the Bay Head Yacht Club, attracted local children who often visited and watched the artist at work.

Jerry married Charlotte Lewis Whitehead in 1905. This late-in-life union, which surprised many, changed his lifestyle, notably by his moving into a large Lake Avenue house owned by her family. They also resided in New York.

Hardenbergh's work is known for landscapes of the surrounding towns and seascapes, typically watercolors that capture the moods of Barnegat Bay. He completed a chart of American birds for Scribner's that was formally endorsed by the American Ornithological Union. Some of his birds were published as color prints and were reproduced on china plates. Hardenbergh, who also drew wrecks, published the print *Wreck of the Lizzie H. Brayton*, a schooner driven aground and broken up in December 1904. A source of Hardenbergh's illustrations and local observations are found in his *Illustrated Description of Bay Head*, published in 1909, but also see Jahn and Pedersen.

BERNARD KELLENYI (C. 1920-2013)

Bernard Kellenyi has enriched the Jersey Shore and the area beyond with a variety of building types and architectural styles. The Atlantic City native came to the Red Bank area as a youth with his family to follow the career of his architect father, Alex.

The elder Kellenyi's local work was the start of an upper-end residential development, Suneagles, in the Eatontown–Tinton Falls area, a project that was supplanted by an expanding Fort Monmouth. After World War II experience as a B-17 pilot, Bernie opened his office in Red Bank, which later expanded into Kellenyi Associates. Modernism was then prevalent, and as he explained, "Every young architect wants to do the newest thing." This included the first sloping glass-walled commercial building, no longer extant, for a Red Bank automobile dealer. Particularly satisfying was his first approach to solar design for a Holmdel residence where the siting of the house was positioned to take advantage of the moving sun.

Educational projects would loom large for the firm, including adaptive use designs such as Brookdale Community College and Christian Brothers Academy, where new compatible construction was later planned to blend stylistically with the old. Their many school projects, including St. Rose in Belmar, had the substance for an office specialty, but Bernie did not wish to preclude other work and found there was interrelated professional stimulation in a variety of building types.

Bernie, who had numerous ecclesiastical projects, was the leading architect for the Roman Catholic Diocese of Trenton (and did work for many other

Bernard Kellenyi's extensive educational oeuvre includes the Pollak Theatre at Monmouth University.

denominations), although later in his career, he noted that changing times no longer gave one firm preference for a diocese's body of work.

Bernie steeped himself in traditional design to serve client need. He went to Colonial Williamsburg to prepare for the Colts Neck municipal complex, which was planned as a small village of coordinated buildings that began with the state police structure. The firm, which also engaged in landscape design, installed the lakes there.

The firm's oeuvre also includes senior housing and healthcare facilities. The Pollak Theatre links a round modern theatre section with a traditional classroom wing at Monmouth University, West Long Branch. Farther south, Kellenyi Associates designed the Expressway Corporate Center in Absecon. The firm, with a wide variety of building types in newer and traditional designs, was led for decades by a skilled practitioner, active in professional circles, who received numerous honors, including election to the American Institute of Architects College of Fellows in 2001.

GUSTAVUS W. PACH (1845-1904)

One of America's preeminent photography studios had roots on the Jersey Shore. There at Long Branch, the Pach brothers produced as an early project one of the region's finest illustrated books.

Gustavus, born in Berlin, immigrated to America with his family, including brothers Morris and Gotthelf, while the three were youths. The three developed an early interest in photography. Gustavus worked while a teen for the leading New York photographer Turner & Company and then was reportedly introduced to the Jersey Shore when he was sent to Toms River to recover from a lung ailment. He and his brother Morris were active photographers there by 1864.

By 1867, Gustavus and Gotthelf were in Long Branch taking orders through another's store and through travels by wagon. Legend claims that while in Long Branch they encountered George W. Childs, Anthony J. Drexel and General Grant, who were impressed with their photography. After the latter inquired about their lack of a permanent place of business, the three, or perhaps only Childs and Drexel, advanced the young men a sum, perhaps $1,500, to open a studio. A former stable was fitted up on the grounds of the oceanfront Continental Hotel. In 1868, J.H. Schenk published his *Album of Long Branch*, a volume of one-page narratives of important sites, each illustrated with a tipped-in Pach photograph. This remarkable book provides early, in-depth insight into the town that had emerged as the most significant on the Jersey Shore. The Pachs also published a long series of stereographic view cards as

Gustavus Pach's New Jersey output had beginnings at this modest Long Branch structure.

they maintained a long-term presence in the city where they later located in the West End section.

Following their success in Long Branch, the brothers opened a branch in nearby Ocean Grove and in numerous college towns, including Princeton and at West Point. Their work on class pictures and portraits of the graduates elevated their reputations. The Pach Brothers Studio, headquartered in New York, became a multigenerational operation.

Gustavus assumed sole ownership of two New Jersey sites, Long Branch and Lakewood, in 1903 but died the next year. A second rich collection of published Pach photographs and the source of the Pachs' fortuitous encounter with the cited men who aided their early business can be found in *Those Innocent Years 1898–1914, Images of the Jersey Shore from the Pach Photographic Collection*, a 1993 work by George H. Moss Jr. and Karen L. Schnitzspahn.

John Frederick Peto (1854-1907)

The John Frederick Peto Studio Museum provides the expected glimpse into the life and work of the noted still-life painter, as well as a remarkable story of historic rediscovery. The building at 102 Cedar Avenue, a key structure in the Island Heights Historic District, offers a rare insight into a significant artist's life and times.

Peto's basic biographical information and early exhibition practices are now well known. Born in Philadelphia, he regularly exhibited at the Pennsylvania Academy of Fine Arts. Peto appears to have studied there, although he is largely self-taught. He met William M. Harnett at the academy, a friend and better-known still-life painter, with whom he was regularly confused and is still compared.

Around 1887, Peto discovered Island Heights, which had been founded as a Methodist camp meeting and later developed into a Philadelphia-influenced resort. There he secured summer employment as a cornet player. During a trip to Cincinnati in 1889, he met and married Christine Pearl Smith and relocated to Island Heights, where he built and reportedly designed the Cedar Avenue residence-studio. He then fell into obscurity. Although Peto regularly received invitations to exhibit at the academy, he did not do so while living on the shore. The Petos took in boarders to supplement an income that had become meager from his failure to sell art. Helen, their only child, was born in 1893.

A visit to the museum will provide full appreciation for Peto's several still-life styles, although one observation will provide insight into his state of mind and loss of appeal. He used banal subject matter, worn and shabby objects that perhaps reflected his unsatisfied personal state.

Peto was best known for trompe l'oeil, or fool the eye painting, where realistic objects appear to be lifted off the canvas, a style for which his elder friend Harnett, who predeceased him in 1892, was the recognized master. Since Peto had become all but forgotten by his death, some forged Harnett's signature over Peto's. Indeed, it was once thought Peto's paintings, typically rendered with a softer, less precise look, constituted a phase of Harnett's career. Peto's family maintained the property after his death as they continued to take boarders.

Peto's first solo exhibition in 1949 was preceded by careful study and analysis by art historian Alfred Frankenstein and conservator Sheldon Keck. They discovered the forged signatures and separated the work of the two colleagues. They noticed that a date appearing in the subject of one painting attributed to Harnett postdated his death. When Frankenstein visited Island Heights, he observed of Peto, "He used a relatively small number of models, some of which are still preserved at Island Heights." Thus, seeing the actual

John Frederick Peto's life and work can be perceived at his studio museum, Island Heights.

20

objects that appear in Peto's still lifes, some of which remain on display, helped discern his work.

Over recent decades, Peto has been exhibited repeatedly and has entered the collections of major museums. From his dismal late-in-life efforts to sell paintings for a few dollars in a local shop, Peto has been elevated to the ranks of America's finest still-life artists. You can perceive his life at the Jersey Shore.

WILLIAM LIGHTFOOT PRICE (1861–1916)

Price, an influential architect with a rising historical reputation in his Philadelphia environs, lists three major Atlantic City hotels on his resume. Since these projects are no longer extant, Price can be easily overlooked on the Jersey Shore.

Price, earlier a carpenter, trained with Addison Hutton. He was a Quaker, as was his Atlantic City client Josiah H. White III (see page 134), and probably used religious affiliations in his early career. An advocate of the ideals of the Arts and Crafts movement, he was a cofounder of the Arts and Crafts community of Rose Valley, outside Philadelphia. Price, a backer of the single-tax proponent Henry George, joined with sculptor Frank Stephens to establish Arden, a single-tax community in Delaware. The National Building Museum in Washington wrote for a 2001–02 exhibition that Price was free to design with considerable originality, as much of his work was for progressive managers of the Pennsylvania Railroad and for self-made industrialists of Philadelphia, Pittsburgh and the Midwest.

In 1902, Price, while he was practicing in the firm of Price and McClanahan, began for White the Marlborough Hotel, Atlantic City's finest to date. Price experimented with new materials, which led to his becoming an early advocate for reinforced concrete, a material he utilized for a separate expansion of the Marlborough; the two were later joined as a single entity. When completed in 1906, the Blenheim was the largest reinforced concrete building in the world.

Price later designed a larger, even grander hotel for White, the Traymore, built next door to the Marlborough-Blenheim, to replace an outmoded frame structure of the same name. Also constructed of reinforced concrete, the Traymore also became the largest of that material. The once-luxurious Traymore was razed in 1972 through three controlled implosions, which were shown in the film *Atlantic City*.

Considering Price's modernistic bent, the Jersey Shore and the country no doubt lost the opportunity for a progression of his design art by virtue of his untimely death.

James Charles Sidney (c. 1819–1881)

While the Methodists founded most Jersey Shore religious retreats, the Presbyterians established one at the southernmost tip of the state. They chose James Charles Sidney, a surveyor, cartographer and architect, to plan Sea Grove.

Born in England, Sidney was in Philadelphia by the early 1840s working as a cartographer. He designed houses later in the decade, many later published in 1850 in his *American Cottage and Villa Architecture*. His affiliations and career were varied. Sidney's accomplishments include a map of twenty miles around Philadelphia, the layout of Woodlawn Cemetery with its twenty miles of walks and the master plan for Fairmount Park.

The community of the Sea Grove Association, founded in 1875, was laid out around Sidney's radial plan that spread out from Pavilion Circle at the intersection of Central and Ocean Avenues. Here Sidney placed the Pavilion, a circular-plan covered amphitheatre without walls, as they were deemed unnecessary for the building's summer use. He designed a number of other buildings, notably John Wanamaker's (see page 54) three-story Italianate cottage with large two-story porches, a number of other cottages, a boathouse and a signal station. To demonstrate that the resort was not exclusively Presbyterian, Sidney, at no cost to the congregation, designed the plans for the Episcopal St. Peter's by the Sea. The Sea Grove community was incorporated in 1878 as Cape May Point.

Sidney spent much of his later career designing public schools for Philadelphia. He died after a fall from the roof of his home at 1422 North Seventeenth Street, Philadelphia.

BUSINESS

James M. Allgor (1847–1934)

Allgor's simple business plan was to move across the Shrewsbury River from Sea Bright to Rumson to open a confectionary/ice cream parlor at the foot of Rumson Road. He suffered the misfortune of a dispute with the local gentry that landed him in the insane asylum.

The home-based shop might have been begrudgingly tolerated in the pre–land use regulation era, but Allgor ran afoul of the bluebloods with plans to install two bowling lanes. After the locals' efforts to clamp down on him, Allgor protested by placing on a clothesline women's underwear with mocking references to his antagonists. The effort resulted in charges of libel. Allgor elevated his protests in the form of "spite fences," such as the illustrated example on the next page. They were carefully painted rants on his socialist and antiestablishment bents. He was jailed for violation of a new ordinance that sanctioned signs only after payment of a license fee. Some signs that were claimed libelous landed him in jail, and although Allgor did not surrender, in 1912, he was sent to the Trenton insane asylum. Some may infer that those who deemed his behavior obnoxious were successful in the vengeful way of having him deemed mentally unbalanced and railroaded into the asylum. Others may simply believe that he was nuts.

Allgor, when he emerged from his earlier stints in custody, published and sold a long series of photographic postcards to support himself.

James Allgor built spite fences as expressions of free speech in run-ins with Rumson authorities. *Courtesy of John Rhody.*

After he lost One Rumson Road in a 1914 sheriff's sale, he appeared to have left the area. Known to have been in the insane asylum in 1920, he passed into obscurity.

RUDOLPH GOLDSCHMIDT (1876-1950)

Although Goldschmidt, a German engineer, may have had little personal presence on the Jersey Shore, he built a radio transmitting tower near Tuckerton that at over eight hundred feet was once the tallest structure in the United States.

Goldschmidt invented a rotating radio-frequency machine known as the Goldschmidt alternator, which was manufactured in Germany and utilized for long-distance communications. The tall transmission towers, which enabled intercontinental communication, were built in Eilvese, Germany, and Little Egg Harbor Township; the local tower was known as Tuckerton for the nearby town. Construction there began in May 1912 and was completed in March 1914. While it is believed that experimental contact was initiated late in 1913, formal opening took place with a ceremonial exchange of messages between President Wilson and Kaiser Wilhelm II on June 19, 1914.

The onset of the Great War brought government scrutiny of activity at Tuckerton in order to preclude its use for German military communication. The government assumed control of the facility after America entered the war in 1917 and mandated that all workers there be members of the United States Navy. This requirement resulted in the enlistment of most of them. The station was seized by the United States as war reparations under the Trading With the Enemy Act and conveyed to the American Radio Company, transactions which are detailed in Ocean County Deeds, Book 525, page 1 for the conveyance to the Alien Property Custodian, and page 4 for the transfer to the American Radio Company. During World War II, the station assumed a new role for the detection of enemy U-boat communications.

Goldschmidt, who had collaborated with Albert Einstein on a new type of hearing aid, immigrated to England in 1934 and remained there until his death.

The tower was taken down on December 28, 1955. Three enormous concrete cubes that held support wires remain in the midst of the Mystic Islands development. Given the prohibitive cost of demolishing reinforced concrete, they will likely remain forever.

GUGLIELMO MARCONI (1874-1937)

Marconi's profile could readily be a long recitation of scientific discovery, but on the Jersey Shore, he is known for two significant sites, one for experimental radio transmission, the other for business development.

Born in Bologna, Italy, and interested in electrical science as a youth, Marconi began laboratory experiments at his father's country estate prior to 1895. By that year, he was able to send wireless signals for a distance of over a mile and a half. In England the next year, he secured the world's first patent for wireless telegraphy as he demonstrated transmissions over increasingly greater distances.

Marconi's 1899 arrival in New York was a trip intended for the use of wireless radio to report progress of the America's Cup races held off Sandy Hook, a happening delayed by the intervention of Admiral George Dewey's celebrated naval parade. Thus, it was the latter event that was the first to be reported by wireless from ship to shore, to a point on the grounds of the Navesink Light Station, or Twin Lights, in the Highlands of Navesink. The races were similarly reported a few days later. Another Marconi coastal accomplishment, albeit some distance to the north in 1903 at Cape Cod, was the first United States to England

Guglielmo Marconi's pioneering communication work is exhibited at Twin Lights, Highlands and Information Age Learning Center, Wall. *Courtesy of Fred Carl.*

wireless transmission, made with a well-publicized message between the President Theodore Roosevelt and the king of England.

Marconi, after organization of the Marconi Wireless Telegraph Company of America, visited the business's American headquarters in 1913, the year it opened. Located in rural Wall Township, the facility was known as Belmar for the nearby post and rail town. As World War I intervened, Marconi was commissioned in Italy's army and served in that country's diplomatic corps, while the Belmar plant was taken over by the United States Navy. This location, recovered by Marconi after the war, was sold to the Radio Corporation of America.

Marconi's numerous honors include co-winner of the 1909 Nobel Prize for Physics and induction to the New Jersey Inventors Hall of Fame. Both Twin Lights and the Belmar facility have long, significant histories beyond the Marconi association. The former is a historic site operated by the State of New Jersey, while the latter is home to a consortium of science-oriented museums overseen by the private, nonprofit organization Information Age Learning Center. Each is a National Historic Landmark and provides Jersey Shore opportunities to study one of the world's greatest inventors.

RAYMOND HOWARD STILLMAN (1890–1973)

While Mark Twain may have encouraged investors to buy land because they are not making more land, Ray Stillman might have disagreed. He was a pioneer in the filling of marsh to make building lots on lagoons.

The Newark native, initially interested in agriculture, took courses at Rutgers in 1915, prior to the purchase of an Eatontown farm and the conduct of a produce business. Having found real estate agents ill-informed on farm property, after he entered the sales field, he specialized in country farms as secondary residences.

On the shore, Stillman developed Shelter Cove on Barnegat Bay in Toms River beginning in 1939. While Stillman was not the first to do so, lagoon building set a pattern for construction that mushroomed after World War II. The small houses, typically the Cape Cod design, erected on small lots with dockage, addressed the 1930s growth of leisure boating, activity that also expanded after the war.

Stillman's model, "The Seafarer," an effectively designed cottage that maximized utility and qualified for Federal Housing Administration Title II loans, sold for $1,950 to $2,950, based on amenities and location.

Stillman, who continued with farms, made his greatest coup in 1942 with the purchase of Fahnestock's "Shadow Brook" (see page 108) for a distressed $25,000. After farm buildings were converted to residences and building lots sold, he profited greatly.

John I. Webb (1808-1895)

Webb's agricultural acumen singlehandedly turned a costly, difficult-to-produce crop into a commonplace pleasure enjoyed by the masses: the cranberry.

Wooden-legged John, as he was known, a native of Holmansville, Jackson Township, was reportedly too poor to obtain credit from a grocery but managed to acquire a piece of swampy bog land where cranberry vines grew. Previously he had gathered wild cranberries, but later he observed that "where the rains had washed down sand upon the old peat bottom, there the vines grew longer and the berries clustered thicker and larger than on the bare muck as it is termed." This discovery motivated John to prepare swampy land by covering it with sand to promote growth of the berries. The enormous increase in production resulted in sales that reportedly made him wealthy and revolutionized cultivation of the crop.

Little is known about John personally, although he did remain in Jackson. His *New Jersey Courier* obituary indicated on March 21, 1895, that land speculation led to the loss of his fortune and resulted in poverty. The October 4, 1885 *New York Times* provided both insight into Webb and a depiction of the growth of the cranberry industry.

ENTERTAINERS

Joseph (1898–1987) and George Albert (1899–1973)

When the Albert brothers sought a rural retreat, they landed at the cultural nexus of the Jersey Shore and the Pine Barrens, as the present Pinelands was formerly called. After their beginnings of merely jamming with friends, they and their followers became a musical institution.

The Alberts lived in a then heavily industrialized Sayreville, Middlesex County, when, according to Book 940, page 270 of Ocean Deeds, Joe made his first purchase in 1933, fifty-six acres near Waretown, for a mere $200. He built a cabin, in time called "The Homeplace," which was used for a hunting lodge. Joe's preference was fox hunting, a sport heavy in maintenance of foxes and hounds. The hunt is virtually orchestrated, the fox keeping pace with the hounds. The sounds are almost musical, individual hounds identifiable by the sounds of their brays.

Joe took what we would call early retirement, relocated there around 1939, when he befriended local animals and lived off the land. Admittedly, feeding the deer ended hunting them. As George visited on weekends, they amused themselves by making music, which after they attracted other local players, evolved into regular Saturday night jamborees. Folk tunes indigenous to the Pines were performed with George playing the obligatory fiddle and Joe playing a washtub bass. The Alberts also drew a listening public, still while in their home. The gatherings, which grew by word of mouth and the power of the press, eventually overwhelmed the place and required a new venue.

Joe and George Albert established a folk cultural tradition that lives on in Waretown at Albert Hall.

Following a lapse of about six months, a rented room in the Waretown Auction provided a second home; the tradition continued there. After that place was destroyed by fire in July 1992, "The Sounds of the Jersey Pines" continued, first in a parking lot and then in a nearby school.

The folk tradition begun by the Alberts reached a juncture that required permanence, which took shape with the formation of the Pinelands Cultural Society, an all-volunteer, tax-exempt organization that built Albert Music Hall; it opened January 9, 1997. Live country, bluegrass and Pinelands music is performed at 7:30 p.m. *every* Saturday night with rare holiday exceptions. Speaking from personal conviction, I urge that, regardless of one's musical preference, the intimacy of live music in a New Jersey cultural setting be experienced at Albert Hall, and at a fraction of the cost of a movie. The society's numerous awards have redeemed the ideals of the Alberts' modest beginnings.

OLIVER DOUD BYRON (1842-1920)

Byron's ties to the Jersey Shore, which run deeper than most of the Long Branch acting colony, stem from his network of investment housing and from a major public benefaction, the founding of a fire company.

Byron, born in Frederick, Maryland, debuted in Baltimore in 1856 and later joined the Richmond Theatre, where he performed with John Wilkes Booth. Following participation with other companies, he joined the celebrated Wallack's company in New York, where he played Shakespearean roles. Later he eschewed high art, opting to employ lowly melodrama to pave his path to success. Byron's signature role was Joe Ferris in the 1871 *Across the Continent*, which played out in the Wild West. According to the October 1872 *Song Journal*, this "dramatization of any dime novel" so pleased audiences that Byron milked it several thousand times for over a quarter-century, playing in every conceivable venue. Heroic characters in melodramatic productions became his métier, despite their lack of cultural stature.

Byron was married to the former Mary Kate Crehan, who performed as Kate O'Neil. They bought in 1875 a no-longer extant Shingle-style summer residence in North Long Branch at 459 Ocean Avenue, known as "Castle Byron." They also acquired upward of thirteen investment properties in that part of the city and in adjoining Monmouth Beach. While the houses have a checkered history as a group, the ownership of the one extant at 476 Neptune Boulevard, alternately named "Byron's Bower" or "Honeysuckle Lodge," inspired William J. Busby to research his presence in the area and write in 2006 *The Oliver Byron Legacy—Showman and Builder*.

Byron's celebrated gift to Long Branch was support for his namesake fire company, the Oliver Byron Engine Company No. 5 at 46 Atlantic Avenue, a presence that keeps his memory alive on the Jersey Shore.

CLARENCE CLEMONS (1942-2011)

While Clemons attained fame as the saxophonist of Springsteen's E-Street Band, in the broader cultural context, the two bridged the racial divide that characterized rock music.

Born in Norfolk, Virginia, Clemons, who was a scholarship player at Maryland State College, now the University of Maryland–Eastern Shore, aspired to a professional football career, plans ended by injury. He deserved

Clarence Clemons the "Big Man" came to prominence as saxophonist in Springsteen's E-Street Band.

his nickname, "Big Man," by his presence at six feet, four inches and 250 pounds. After he received an alto saxophone at age nine, he later switched to tenor, and although he grew up immersed in soul music, he envisioned himself a rock musician. Clemons, who was a presence in the black music scene on Asbury Park's West Side, met Springsteen in 1971 in an encounter steeped in Jersey Shore musical lore. While Springsteen was playing a gig at the Student Prince on Kingsley Avenue during a stormy night, Clemons entered to invite himself on the stage to play. The musical attraction was instantaneous; the relationship became profound. As Springsteen attested after Clemons' death, "He was my great friend, my partner, and with Clarence at my side, my band and I were able to tell a story far deeper than those simply contained in our music."

Clemons's music making later focused in Red Bank, where in the early 1980s, he owned the rock club Big Man's West. According to the June 19, 2011 *New York Times*, he recorded a number of hits individually, acted in both films and television and had a celebrated jam session with President Bill Clinton at his 1993 inaugural ball.

JOSEPHINE SHAW HOEY (1824–1896)

There was a second act in the career of Mrs. Hoey, as she was widely called after her second marriage. An emigrant from Liverpool with her musician-poet father, John, she first appeared on the stage in Baltimore as a teen.

Josephine was married in 1847 to W.H. Russell, treasurer of Burton's National Theatre, New York, where she performed. During a stage run, she was apparently courted from the audience by John Hoey (see page 126). After they married in 1849, she retired for a spell but was lured back to the boards by James Wallack, an actor, owner of Wallack's Theatre and a figure also associated with the Jersey Shore. She reigned as his leading lady.

Contemporary criticism varied, but it is apparent that Hoey possessed a restrained, dignified beauty. A *Daily Graphic* reporter reflected her stature when he noted on July 21, 1878, that she "has given Long Branch its distinctive character as a home for managers and actors." At a time when performers provided their own costumes, the Hoeys' generous budget permitted her to dress lavishly. Hoey was credited for setting a trend for fancy performance attire.

Hoey retired permanently in 1865, when she presumably led a comfortable domestic lifestyle. Their personal routines were overturned by John's business fiscal entanglement. She held title to their mansion at the southwest corner of Fifth Avenue and 22nd Street, New York, which apparently did not safeguard the property as it was reportedly transferred to Adams Express in her husband's settlement.

MADAME MARIE (c. 1915–2008)

Her surname, hardly known until her death in 2008, was virtually immaterial as Madam Marie had attained single-name fame and recognition, aided by her iconic shed on the Asbury Park boardwalk.

The fortune-telling career of Marie Castello began in the 1930s. While the origin of her booth, also known as the Temple of Knowledge, located adjacent to the landmark Convention Hall is obscure, she was reportedly the longest-tenured tenant on the boardwalk. Her notoriety soared in 1973, when Bruce Springsteen mentioned her in a lyric. What the song's words about being "busted" lacked in accuracy, they made up in fame-propelling power. When Madam Marie told his fortune, she claimed he would be a

Madame Marie's Temple of Knowledge not only endures after her passing, but is also an iconic symbol of the Asbury Park boardwalk.

success. Springsteen jokingly dismissed her prediction with the belief that she said that to all the musicians, but he continued to acknowledge her. One of Madam Marie's predictions was for the rise of Asbury Park, not a difficult one as she saw the depths to which the city had sunk. A relative's ability to continue the operation was also predictable, as the Madam Marie brand and the Temple of Knowledge endure.

Arthur Pryor (1870-1942)

Before "Asbury Park sound" entered the popular lexicon, there was Arthur Pryor, who built an Asbury Park musical tradition. His career based at the Jersey Shore established him as an American popular music icon.

Pryor was born in St. Louis and raised in St. Joseph, Missouri, by a bandleader father and pianist mother. His earliest success was as a virtuoso trombone prodigy, which earned him selection for John

Arthur Pryor, a renowned bandleader who led his group for three decades, created the original Asbury Park sound.

Philip Sousa's band and legendary stature with that instrument. Pryor stayed with Sousa, rising to assistant conductor, until his father's 1902 death, when the son assumed direction of and then reorganized the original Pryor Band. In November 1903, Arthur debuted in New York, prior to his first appearance in Asbury Park the next summer. There he established himself as the musical highlight and endured for three decades. He also conducted and arranged for the Victor Talking Machine Company.

Pryor composed an extensive and varied body of music, notably marches and band numbers, but also three light operas, tone poems and solo pieces for trombone. Three of his best-known pieces were "The Whistler and His Dog," "On Jersey Shore" and "Queen Titania," the latter composed in conjunction with the Asbury Park baby parade.

While Pryor never stopped playing, he announced his intended retirement in 1933, the year he made a successful run for public office, as he was elected to the Monmouth County Board of Chosen Freeholders in that November's Democratic sweep. However, he was defeated in a reelection try in 1936. Pryor, who married the former Maude Russell, had three sons, including Roger Pryor who was both bandleader and film actor. Following Arthur's having played at a war bond rally in the spring of 1942, he was engaged for a series of concerts scheduled to have begun on July 4, but he died on June 18 at his West Long Branch home. By then, he had become a Jersey Shore legend.

DAN RICE (1823-1900)

His biography is titled *Dan Rice: The Most Famous Man You've Never Heard Of.* How did this enormously popular performer rise to fame and then fall into obscurity? Dan Rice was a clown, but not the silent, evil, cartoonish figure to which the role has devolved. The clown, especially as embodied by Rice, was a major entertainer, who not only used a voice but also commented on the issues of the day.

Rice, born Daniel McLaren in New York to parents perhaps not united by matrimony, their union broken up by his maternal grandfather, was raised in the Long Branch area by his mother, Elizabeth Rice. Leaving home as a youth to seek a showman's career, he arrived in Pittsburg employing a trained pig act. Rice would develop a diverse repertoire that included singing, strongman acts and narration. He organized a circus, dubbed "Dan Rice's Great Show," so-named as the term "circus" at the time was typically understood to be a building rather than an act, while circus performances were "equestrian exhibitions." The Rice clown figure was attired in what became recognized as an "Uncle Sam" suit, although he did not originate the figure. His clown persona was fixed as a serious social and political commentator, one engaged in discussion with an interactive audience. Crowds of the day could be rough, even violent, which resulted in not infrequent fisticuffs by the pugnacious Rice, whose life was marked by a trail of fighting and litigation. He also billed himself a humorist.

Rice's popularity and fame soared. He built a winter headquarters and mansion in Girard, Pennsylvania, then on centrally located highways. A politically active Democrat, he ran unsuccessfully for that state's senate in 1864. His later aspirations for higher office were pipe dreams. While

Dan Rice, who elevated the clown role into serious social commentator, built and lost three fortunes.

Rice reached the peak of his success then, securing financing for his shows became difficult. By the 1870s, work became spotty and alcoholism a challenge. He lectured in the next decade, but life was often a struggle. Rice was married four times; his first wife ran off with one of his business officials and started a competing circus. He built and lost three fortunes.

Rice, broke and broken, returned to Monmouth County in the 1890s, where he was taken in by Maria Ward Brown at her 262 Norwood Avenue home in what is now West Long Branch. The myths about his career, which began in his lifetime, were later fueled by Rice in his memoirs, which were dictated to Brown, who self-published *The Life of Dan Rice* the year after his death. She became embittered by the book's lack of success. The flawed work suffers from the subject's exaggeration and fabrication. David Carlyon's thoroughly researched 2001 biography, noted in the lead-in, is the authoritative source. Although Rice's recognition has risen lately on the shore, he is revered in Girard, where the town commemorates him with an annual summer celebration.

NATHAN SALSBURY (1846–1902)

Nathan Salsbury's beginning, as the Illinois native told it, was his enlistment in the Union Army while a boy, a role in which he served multiple tours, the second following his having been mustered out after being wounded. He claimed to have left the army with $20,000, largely winnings at poker.

Nate recalled how the warmth of his personality and ability to entertain at war camps lifted soldiers' spirits. His reflections included a recounting of a theatrical life that had a lowly stage start in Grand Rapids, Michigan, one that was resurrected with a four-year run as a comedian at the Boston Museum. He found his true métier following his founding the Salsbury Troubadours, a traveling company that toured both sides of the Atlantic. While with the Troubadours, Salsbury met William Cody; the two launched "Buffalo Bill's Wild West Show," Salsbury's greatest success. The well-traveled Salsbury, in need of a home base, found Long Branch through regular visits with Frank Maeder, his manager. In 1882, he bought a Liberty Street lot that adjoined Maeder's; Salsbury's house does not survive. However, memory of Salsbury has endured on the Jersey Shore as a consequence of investment property.

In 1900, Salsbury purchased the former site of the East End Hotel, a 16.66-acre plot in North Long Branch that suffered from neglect. He divided

THE PERSONALITIES & POLITICS THAT BUILT AMERICA'S RESORT

it into fourteen lots to form a housing colony known as "The Reservation." Nine of the eleven houses planned were built, most located east of Ocean Avenue and each given an Indian name. Salsbury did not live to enjoy the fruits of his investment.

The buildings were regularly buffeted by storms while their exposed locations required considerable upkeep. In time, all except "The Navaho" were lost. The property, which had a checkered history in the 1960s–70s, was acquired by the County of Monmouth, which turned it into their Seven Presidents Park. This beachfront location is the most visited site in the Monmouth County Park System's extensive network and a reminder of a great theatrical producer.

BRUCE SPRINGSTEEN (B. 1949)

While Springsteen, born in Long Branch, raised in Monmouth County's inland county seat Freehold and now resident of Rumson and Colts Neck, enjoys worldwide stature, the Jersey Shore has regularly been a presence in his illustrious career.

Springsteen's first band, the Castiles, formed at Freehold High School, played at smaller, local venues including beach clubs, while a second band, Steel Mill, had a strong presence at Monmouth College (now University). His first commercially successful group, the E-Street Band, was named for the Belmar location of an original member's home and their rehearsal space.

Asbury Park, an early and continued presence for Springsteen, dated from his early observations of the black musicians on the city's segregated west side. He would listen from the sidewalk at a time when he was too young for admission to the sites. The 1973 *Greetings from Asbury Park* was his first album to attract significant industry notice; two years later, major celebrity followed with the enormous success of *Born to Run*. Claims that Springsteen's stardom was foreordained are reinforced by the realization that biographer Peter Ames Carton uncovered the first time Bruce was called "the Boss": it was in 1971 in an apartment on the edge of downtown Asbury Park. The long-popular Asbury Park musical tradition (see Arthur Pryor, page 33) accelerated and reinvented itself with a major rock-and-roll revival in the 1960s. The first Bruce venue in the city was the Upstage club late in that decade. Bruce is linked with the Stone Pony, although he has not been officially booked there. However, impromptu jam and rehearsal sessions at the Stone Pony and the Wonder Bar are legendary among Bruce buffs. Rumors of an anticipated appearance will still send hoards of the hopeful crowding the streets eager for a glimpse and listening experience. Bruce is associated with Convention Hall, the storied landmark of the Asbury Park music scene, through various earlier performances. Famously, he launched from there the heavily promoted and enormously successful 2000–03 tour following the release of *The Rising*, his greatest twenty-first-century success to date.

After Bruce lived for a spell in Long Branch, the rented house virtually became a local landmark. Fan interest, almost obsession, extends to any of his former domiciles, even the dining places he favors or other sites with personal associations.

Springsteen's career has become the subject of academic symposia, notably at Monmouth University, a reflection of Bruce's penetration into the heart of American cultural history. I have seen one of their breakout walking tours in Freehold, a pack soaking up his youthful environs. Freehold should not be overlooked, as Bruce, who lived within a block of his St. Rose of Lima church, later "realized, as time passed, that my music is filled with Catholic imagery." His lyrics also include numerous local references. Glenn LeBoeuf, organizer of BruceTours, which offers guided tours of sites associated with Springsteen, told me, "There is an insatiable interest in all places tied to Springsteen, not only where he lived and performed, but where he ate and hung out."

An enormous body of literature on Springsteen composes the archival Bruce Springsteen Special Collection at Monmouth University. Curator Eileen Chapman, who generously helped with the Springsteen profile, points out that the archive is a major draw for scholars from all over the world who show particular interest in the major items that have propelled his career.

GORDON TURK (B. 1949)

Summertime organ concerts in Ocean Grove's Great Auditorium are a musical highlight of the Jersey Shore experience. They are but one activity in the varied career of the Grove's resident organist, Dr. Gordon Turk.

The son of a New Jersey minister, Gordon, who trained at the Curtis Institute of Music, Philadelphia, and the Manhattan School of Music, resides in St. David, Pennsylvania, but spends summers in Ocean Grove, where

Gordon Turk, a scholarly musician and director of the Ocean Grove music program, is heard on the organ every summer week in the Great Auditorium.

he administers an extensive music program. He also teaches, formerly as professor of organ at West Chester University and of publication at Rowan University. Gordon has won organ competitions, including the performance of the music of Johann Sebastian Bach and organ improvisation for the American Guild of Organists.

Ocean Grove was founded as a camp meeting grounds by the Methodists (see Ellwood H. Stokes, page 138). Regarding that religious background, Gordon pointed out that "the spirit is in the bones of the place. Ocean Grove is a great place to come together for Sunday services. The spirit is still felt in the music, especially the great old Methodist hymns." The instrument and venue are landmarks of musical and architectural history. The organ, built by the firm of Robert Hope Jones and first played in 1908, contains over eleven thousand pipes. It is one of the greatest organs in America. The Great Auditorium, a massive wood structure erected in 1894 on a steel frame, is the key building in the Grove, where the entire town is a National Register Historic District.

Off season, Gordon is the organist and choirmaster at St. David's Episcopal Church, Wayne, Pennsylvania. He has toured, playing across the United States and in Europe and Japan.

FOUNDERS

Captain John Arnold (1818–1886)

The namesake of Arnold Avenue, familiar as the main business stem of Point Pleasant Beach, also deserves recognition, as Captain John Arnold was one of the greatest benefactors of a Jersey Shore town.

Born near the present Deal, Monmouth County, John relocated to the Point Pleasant area around 1820, when his mother, widowed before his birth, married Thomas Cook (see page 43). At fourteen, he was employed in a New York pharmacy, which he later purchased. Arnold claimed to have made a tidy sum during the 1834–35 cholera epidemic from selling a "salubrious" root beer of his own making. After he found the pharmacy business confining, John took to the sea, became a ship owner and engaged in maritime affairs for over two decades before he returned to the future Point Pleasant Beach, a region then still in a state of wilderness.

John built a large boarding establishment, the Arnold House. He acquired extensive landholdings but sold some with the thought of future development. One tract was early known as Arnold City. He founded White Lawn Cemetery in 1874. His greatest public benefaction was having induced the New York and Long Branch Railroad to extend their line from Sea Girt to Point Pleasant Beach, accomplished through his providing land and funds. Arnold also convinced the Counties of Monmouth and Ocean to bridge the Manasquan River, which became a major enhancement of road travel. Arnold also had an interest in the development of Mantoloking.

One can later readily enumerate the accomplishments of a public-minded citizen, but the mark of his esteem was the heartfelt testaments at his passing from a grateful populace.

BAKER BROTHERS: PHILIP PONTIUS (1846-1920); JACOB THOMPSON (1847-1919); LATIMER (1849-1932)

The Baker brothers—in Wildwood, they are frequently mentioned as a group—who came from Lewisburg, Pennsylvania, to Five Mile Beach, transformed their holdings from a wild and desolate beach to an intensively developed vacation and amusement district.

The Bakers, all born on a farm in Cowan, Union County, Pennsylvania, separated in their early careers. Philip and Latimer located in Vineland, Cumberland County, in 1869 to open the mercantile business, Baker Brothers, while J. Thompson practiced law in Lewisburg. In 1885, they bought an extensive tract on Five Mile Beach, named, as were a number of the Jersey Shore barrier islands, for its length. Early descriptions of the area characterize this difficult environment as largely scrub pines, other trees and sand dunes. Indeed, the name "Wildwood" has its origin from the land. Utilizing the same Baker Brothers style for their real estate business, they began the slow, steady sale of lots as they laid out streets. Growth would be aided by the arrival of the railroad.

The Bakers were not the first on the island, as others were able to incorporate Holly Beach in 1885. Anglesea, a small fishing village at the island's northernmost end, was incorporated in 1895, the same year as Wildwood.

The Bakers began their political activity with Philip's 1882 election to the state assembly; the state senate followed in 1886. Each would be elected to a mayoralty on the island. Latimer became Wildwood's first mayor at its 1895 incorporation, while in 1912, J. Thompson became the first mayor of Wildwood following its merger with Holly Beach. Philip, the active force in the development of Wildwood Crest, which is south of Wildwood, was chosen its first mayor in 1912, a post he held until his death.

The brothers engaged in various business ventures, including the Wildwood Title and Trust Company and the Wildwood and Delaware Short Line. They also held various civic-charitable positions. Philip, the moving force behind the establishment of the New Jersey Training School for Feeble-Minded Children in Vineland, served as board president for thirty years. The three not only built the Wildwoods, but for the rest of their lives they were also the moving forces for their betterment. J. Thompson's residence at 3008 Atlantic Avenue in Wildwood, now owned by the Wildwood Civic Club, was entered on the National Register of Historic Places in 1996, largely for its association with his daughter Katherine (see page 146).

JAMES ADAM BRADLEY (1830–1921)

After Bradley discovered a coastal wilderness, he possessed the foresight to develop Asbury Park as a great Jersey Shore resort. After Bradley was overtaken by changing times, his sale of key holdings enabled the acceleration of the city's growth.

Born in Rossville, Staten Island, and raised in Manhattan, Bradley began working as a youth prior to becoming a successful brush manufacturer in lower Manhattan. Overwork brought him to Methodist Ocean Grove, where Bradley, also a Methodist, embraced the concept of a healthy resort organized on Christian, temperance and clean-living values. Learning that a large tract of rough, unsettled but unspoiled land to its north was available, Bradley purchased five hundred acres.

Bradley, impossible to characterize briefly, possessed a vision that established his conceived resort, which rapidly grew and prospered. Bradley instilled his values through close, personal scrutiny and deed restrictions that barred the gambling and alcohol that made nearby Long Branch the antithesis of his aspirations. His bigotry may be at the root of racial discord that erupted in riots in 1970, cleaving wounds still not fully healed.

James A. Bradley, the founder of Asbury Park, was a visionary but became frustrated by changing times.

Bradley's 1903 sale to the city of the beachfront unleashed bonds that accelerated the resort's prosperity; it also signaled that his time had passed. His interest diminished, he endured nearly twenty years. He was aware of the city's plans to honor him with a statue but passed three weeks prior to its unveiling.

THOMAS COOK JR. (c. 1792–1874)

While Uncle Tommy Cook left a scant biography, he was legendary as the keeper of what was arguably the oldest boardinghouse in the future Point Pleasant Beach.

Cook's father acquired the first piece of an eventual three-hundred-acre farm in 1782 and built the famed house not long thereafter. Early records lack specificity, but it is believed that the family took in boarders around the 1820s. The place, an active producing farm, was also dotted with a number of outbuildings. The younger Cook is recorded in rescue annals for his vivid testimony after the February 1846 tragic wreck of the *John Minturn* in which nearly all of the fifty-one passengers and crew plus twenty seamen taken from an earlier wreck were killed, many frozen to death during vain waits for rescue.

Cook attracted a large and loyal following. The *New York World* reported on August 10, 1885, that farmers from northern New Jersey and Pennsylvania, who traveled to the shore in summer to clam and fish, boarded there. Their guest register included the names of Commodore Stockton, former governor Joel Parker and others with national reputations. One couple had not missed a visit in thirty-five years.

The farm was acquired by the River and Oceanfront Land Improvement Company in 1902. Development followed, while the house stood until destruction by fire in 1942.

EDWARD S. FARROW (1855–1926)

Farrow's vision for the Jersey Shore was an ambitious plan to build a Berkeley Township retirement community for military officers. His contentious personality and controversial style often ensnared him in litigation. The legal imbroglio that emerged from his efforts to establish this town was a factor that led to its failure. However, Farrow's stature stems from a long, distinguished career with the military, first in uniform as an Indian fighter and later in life with industry as a World War I munitions developer.

Farrow, born in Maryland to a physician who served in the Civil War and a member of the United States Military Academy Class of 1876, served with distinction in the Indian campaigns, the source of his first book, *Mountain Scouting—A Handbook for Officers and Soldiers on the Frontier*. Lieutenant Farrow was assigned to West Point as an instructor on infantry and artillery tactics. His prolific writings include *Farrow's Military Encyclopedia*, *Dictionary of Military Terms*, *Of Riots and Riot Duty* and *Gas Warfare*.

After Farrow resigned his commission on February 24, 1892, he remained allied with the government for much of his career. He appears to have discovered the Jersey Shore while acting as director of surveys in the Barnegat Bay section of New Jersey while still in uniform. His plans for the retirement community began to take shape after he bought a 4,070-acre tract near Bayville in 1886 on which he laid out a 300-acre residential section in 1887, reserving the remainder for hunting and recreational purposes. Farrow organized the Barnegat Bay Company and then named the settlement Barnegat Park, which he promoted as "The New Army and Navy Seaside Home." While the military was his target market, lots were also sold to other "acceptable persons" for a small cash deposit with the balance due in monthly or quarterly payments. Farrow publicized his venture in the *Barnegat Park News*, which published military articles but was effectively a house organ. The development attracted many buyers, although no attempt has been made to ascertain which had a military background. A number of houses were built at the time as the nascent community attracted a bank, post office and the railroad. In addition, Farrow built a store and a large hotel named The Pines.

Farrow's many complicated real estate transactions often were in the name of his associate John B. Larner. The underfinanced venture, bankrupt by 1892, immersed Farrow in litigation issues that resulted in trial by court-martial, a struggle he overcame after it was ascertained that the case was not a military matter. After a suspicious fire destroyed most of the public buildings on October 21, 1893, another blaze burned The Pines on July 5, 1895. While Farrow remained committed as a resident, he sought rescue as early as 1905 when he enlisted the Baker brothers, (see page 41), the successful developers of the Wildwoods. However, the eventual Great War and a dearth of buyers doomed those plans.

Farrow's munitions expertise gave him an active weapons development role during the Great War; he is credited with a number of inventions. He prepared textbooks and assisted in the education and training of the new army. He also offered for free his Barnegat Park estate for military purposes. He later placed his trust to resurrect Barnegat Park with banker Benjamin W. Sangor, who after Farrow's death undertook ambitious plans, which included a new hotel. These, too, collapsed as Sangor was jailed for fraud. Eventually, the Pinewald section of Berkeley emerged from the fiscal maelstrom.

Edward S. Farrow's military retirement home failed, but the Pinewald community emerged from it. *Courtesy of United States Military Academy Library, Special Collections.*

JAMES V. LAFFERTY JR. (1858–1898)

In 1881, Lafferty sought to draw attention to his new real estate development of marginal lots on an Absecon Island tract south of Atlantic City. His grand idea created an unusual structure that was intended to serve as a restaurant. It became the region's iconic symbol and is now called Lucy the Elephant.

Born in Philadelphia of prosperous Irish immigrants, Lafferty fashioned himself an engineer and inventor. Lafferty engaged Philadelphia architect William Free to help create his conception, to be built on a frame of rugged twelve by twelve timbers, and then Joseph Mason Kirby for its construction. Erecting the sixty-five-foot-high, or about six-story, tin-clad beast was budgeted for a then substantial $25,000, but costs ran upward of $38,000.

Lafferty realized that his creation was unique, so in June 1882, he applied for a patent for buildings shaped like animals, what is now called zoomorphic architecture, which was granted that December. Two other elephants followed in 1885: the enormous Elephant Colossus, built in Coney Island at 122 feet, and Cape May's Light of Asia at 40 feet. Neither is extant, the former having burned in 1896, while the latter fell to neglect and vandalism.

The elephant helped spark interest in an area that was little more than scrub pine and sand dunes. The resultant growth prompted the incorporation of South Atlantic City in 1885, which changed its name to Margate in 1909. However, Lafferty's venture declined, which resulted in its sale to Anton Gertzen of Philadelphia in 1887. It is believed that the name Lucy was given during Gertzen's ownership, perhaps by a daughter-in-law. Its naming was not impeded by the figure's male characteristic tusks.

Over the decades, Lucy's checkered existence threatened the structure, which by the 1960s declined to a precarious state. Determined to be structurally sound, the building was moved in 1970 two blocks south to 9200 Atlantic Avenue as part of a Save Lucy campaign. The ensuing restoration permitted tours by 1974, while in 1976, Lucy was designated a National Historic Landmark. Preserving Lucy is ongoing. After researching and designing the reconstruction of the original interior, Lucy's distinguished preservation architect Margaret Westfield

James F. Lafferty is remembered by his Lucy the Elephant structure, which endures as an iconic symbol of the Jersey Shore.

has had to deal with two lightning strikes, a broken tusk and extensive material deterioration.

Lafferty's elephantine creation, designed as a real estate draw, has become his personal historical monument.

ADMIRAL ELIE A.F. LAVALLETTE (1790–1862)

One can only speculate if Admiral Lavallette ever visited the Jersey Shore, but his interest stems from his status as the namesake of a Squan Beach borough, an honor bestowed by his developer son.

When he was born in Alexandria, Virginia, his French-extraction family spelled their name La Vallette. After Elie entered the navy in 1812, he saw action at the crucial American victory of the Battle of Lake Champlain and then after the war was assigned command of a coastal survey vessel in 1817. Thirty years later, Lavallette had Mexican War activity off the Gulf of California, while after the war he became military governor of Mazatlan.

The admiral's son Albert T. was a vice-president of the Philadelphia-based Barnegat Land Improvement Company, which laid out a tract originally called Lavallette City-by-the-Sea. Their 1880 advertisement wrote glowingly: "It contains 500 acres of land, having about two miles of seafront and an unequalled beach of hard, unyielding sand, inclining gently towards the sea, from which there is no perceptible undertow." The area was incorporated as a borough in 1887. The sand actually did yield under storm conditions.

CHARLES LOVELAND (1796–?)

In 1837, Charles Loveland, born in Mount Holly, was the first of the family to settle near what had been Herberts Creek and is now the Point Pleasant Canal in the northern section of the Borough of Point Pleasant. Thus, he may be the founder of Lovelandtown. However, was that a place or a name that entered public cognizance only after the construction of the Lovelandtown Bridge?

John was not the first to settle the area that Stouts and Johnsons already called home. The family acquired an extensive tract over time and populated the region with Lovelands, who embraced life on the bay. They built a number of residences, along with a carriage house and boathouse.

Lovelands were gunners, ship captains, decoy carvers and renters of rooms to bay sport enthusiasts.

A locality as a place, as opposed to a municipality, should have a recorded form of public recognition. These include contemporary usage, a public facility, e.g. school, church or station that embraces the name. Still better is location on a map from the times. Nothing has been found despite Esther Loveland Kinsey's claimed recollection of an 1890 map. While Pauline S. Miller's 1993 *Lovelandtown—A Small Hamlet in Ocean County, New Jersey* depicts in a charming manner the memories of times past, the key issue of period public recognition is unaddressed.

The prominent "Lovelandtown Bridge" sign at the Highway 88 crossing of the canal often prompts some to wonder "just where is Lovelandtown." Historians still search for evidence that Lovelandtown was a place in its time.

Great John Mathis (c. 1690-1779)

The name Great John Mathis always attracts attention for the obvious— "great" preceding the given name. Although the term was a general honorific for distinguished men, one can measure John's stature with the rarity of that appellation. He was the major figure in Bass River Township history and effectively established Little Egg Harbor Township.

Details on John's early life are obscure. Born around 1690 in Wales, he arrived in Oyster Bay, New York, sometime in the early eighteenth century. In 1713, he bought 250 acres of Bass River Township marshland known as Bisbees or Oak Island with two partners whom he bought out the next year when he relocated to Little Egg Harbor Township. John bought numerous tracts of land in the region and at an unknown date changed his surname from Mathews to Mathis; he was still identified as the former in a 1746 New Jersey deed.

John owned multiple farms. He bought his second in 1729 and built his family's residence not long thereafter. Located in the area of today's Mathistown Road, the house was destroyed in the Revolution. John was married to the widow Alice Andrews Higbee, the daughter of Edward Andrews. Andrews was a substantial citizen who built a gristmill in 1704, donated land in 1709 for the Quaker Meetinghouse and bequeathed his daughter an unspecified sum, which no doubt aided the investments of her husband. John was a shipbuilder who may have been active in the West Indies trade. When banking was personal, he was a major lender and held numerous mortgages.

BERTRAM CHAPMAN MAYO (1865-1920)

Bertram C. Mayo is esteemed in the Borough of Beachwood, Ocean County, as their founding father. Examination of his promotional practices suggests that he may have been a charlatan and a crook. Which was he, founder or fraud, or was he both?

One could claim that Mayo had a national operation in view of land promotional ventures in California and Michigan. However, he distanced himself from each as his deceptive modus operandi resulted in disappointment at best, but often outrage. Mayo engaged newspapers to promote subscriptions through the offering of lots that were ostensible bargains but in reality had little value. Sales were generated through hyperbolic promotion.

At Beachwood, Mayo's partner, or rather tool, the *New York Tribune* began offering in 1914 a lot for only $19.60 to purchasers of a six-month subscription. The prospect saw appealing brochures and advertisements that portrayed an improved waterfront locale on Toms River, one built with recreational facilities, including a yacht club and community clubhouse, fine streets and a station on the Central Railroad. They actually existed but were accessible to few.

The area, known in real estate circles as the "2,000 Acre Tract," was in reality a dismal expanse of scrub pine, which was transferred anonymously in order to conceal the ultimate owner. Surprises awaited eager *Tribune* customers. City folks easily reached the site on the railroad but soon realized that their lots were not near the water but were in the undeveloped pines west of the rail line. In addition, adequate safe railroad crossings did not exist. They also learned that in order to build, multiple lots were needed; the rest were available at regular prices. The yacht club was a small boathouse.

Beachwood buyers were resilient. In 1916, they formed a borough by

Revered in Beachwood, Mayo has a mixed record. Read his profile to determine if he was founder or fraud. *Courtesy of Ocean County Historical Society.*

separating from Dover Township and then took measures for raising their community. A memorial tribute after Mayo's untimely death claimed, "In this noble work, he was a benefactor to the human race and thousands in Beachwood and other summer resorts already rise up and call him blessed." While we respect the dead and Beachwood still acclaims him, the underside of his practices, once lost to history, reveal the dismal early scenario. The source is congressional hearings in 1916 investigating charges against Judge H. Snowden Marshall, apparently for conduct in *Mayo-Tribune* litigation proceedings. Obviously the town rallied around its own, but be assured that Mayo was no benefactor.

MICHAEL L. ORTLEY (1795–1843)

While Ortley Beach, the prominent oceanfront section of Toms River Township is well known, its familiarity increased after the area was devastated during Hurricane Sandy. However, its namesake has rested in historic obscurity. Regional sporting activity there preceded the area's residential settlement.

Ortley Beach embraces the site of the former Cranberry Inlet, which was once located about opposite Toms River. This former outlet to the sea closed in 1812. The appearances of Michael Ortley in historical references typically relate to his long, difficult, costly efforts to reopen the inlet, work that the New Jersey Legislature sanctioned in 1816. He managed to accomplish his goal in 1820, but success lasted for merely a single day. The powerful sea closed the inlet by the morning after its opening. This venture reportedly impoverished Ortley, although he remained "land rich," still in possession of a lengthy tract along the barrier beach. The ocean's enduring influence resulted in an 1862 suit by Ortley's widow, Axsea, to settle a border dispute.

Ortley's land drew gunning parties, typically urban residents who enjoyed shore recreation. The best description of the place was penned by a gunner with the nom de plume "Widgeon," who recalled from his youth the extensive tract of "Mammy Ortley," which extended from Chadwick Beach to the site of the former inlet. He wrote in the November 1917 *Forest and Stream* that he remembered an old house that apparently had seen better days, surrounded by tall willows and two large silver maples, the only trees on Squan Beach, which coastal schooner captains used for reckoning their position. "The long stretch of Ortley's beach had many noted shooting points on the bay," each with a specific name.

Widgeon claimed that the coming of the railroad marred the area for shooting. After the widow Ortley died in 1875, the land passed to the heirs, which included at least three sons and two daughters, and was eventually sold for development.

Recent deed research has placed a different perspective on Ortley's activity. Monmouth Deeds Book Y, page 847, reveals that Ortley's first purchase was in 1816. Thus, his exertions to reopen the inlet were apparently not efforts to secure or improve existing holdings, but rather a speculative venture. Ortley learned that real estate speculation, of course, is not always profitable.

Dr. Jonathan Pitney (1797-1869)

Dr. Pitney had a vision to organize a health resort on Absecon Island. The fulfillment of that ideal made him "the father of Atlantic City."

Born in Mendham, New Jersey, Pitney studied medicine at Columbia and practiced on Staten Island for two years prior to his 1820 relocation to a sparsely settled section of the southern shore that was still part of Gloucester County. There he began his long-lasting practice of medicine. Pitney's long résumé in public life included advocacy for the 1837 organization of Atlantic County, delegate to the state's 1844 Constitutional Convention, Absecon postmaster in 1847 and an unsuccessful run for Congress in 1848. As an early advocate for a lighthouse at the Absecon Inlet, Pitney petitioned Congress in 1837. The light, after numerous delays and shipwrecks, was finally first lit on January 15, 1857.

Forming a resort on isolated, virtually uninhabited Absecon Island would need to overcome a great challenge—creating a way to get there. Pitney enlisted another visionary, Philadelphia civil engineer Richard B. Osborne, who had observed the creation of Chicago and the emergence of towns in the Midwest. The two would convince investors that the Jersey Shore presented an opportunity to profit.

The sandy pinelands across southern New Jersey made for a difficult stagecoach ride but proved an easy environment for laying railroad track. The Camden and Atlantic Railroad was the first to enter the planned city that Osborne laid out. The short ferry ride to the Camden western rail terminus from Philadelphia made Atlantic City a Philadelphia resort. The rail line opened in 1854, the first of a future web of rail connections along the Jersey Shore. The at first steady, then rapid growth of Atlantic City gave form to what became "America's Favorite Playground."

Vision for a shorefront health resort made Dr. Pitney "the father of Atlantic City." His residence is now an inn.

After Dr. Pitney's home on the mainland on Route 9 was threatened with destruction in 1995, two men rescued it for conversion into a bed-and-breakfast inn. It remains so at publication.

EBENEZER TUCKER (1758–1845)

Ebenezer Tucker is the second family member to leave his name on the map but the only one that is retained. Naming Tuckerton was a deserved honor considering his lifelong work to raise the fortunes of the Little Egg Harbor area.

Ebenezer's father, Reuben, who emigrated from New York State, bought what became Tuckers Beach in the eighteenth century and was known as Long Beach in the nineteenth. There may be a question on when he acquired the tract, but over time, its southern tip separated as an island before it submerged totally. Tuckers Island is gone.

Barber and Howe, in their 1845 *Historical Collections of the State of New Jersey*, wrote that Ebenezer settled in 1778 at "Middle of the Shore," located on the

Ebenezer Tucker, the namesake of Tuckerton and benefactor to the town in many ways, is represented by his impressive monument.

mainland opposite the southern shore of Long Beach, a place later known as Clamtown. After the Revolution, during which Tucker served in the army, he purchased land there, sold lots for development and engaged in shipping and mercantile activity. The area, which had been a hotbed of privateer activity during the war, became an early port of entry in 1791, when Ebenezer was appointed collector. Tucker's other positions included long-term service on the bench, two terms in Congress and appointment as the town's first postmaster. He was esteemed for his public spirit and benefactions.

The precise timing of the renaming of Clamtown is in question at publication. The longtime local belief is the year 1798, depicted in Blackman's history, although Barber and Howe claimed it was 1786. The

Tuckerton post office was established in 1797, while port of entry directives in 1796 referred to Tuckerton. On March 3, 1791, the *Burlington Advertiser* reported the brig *Betsey* wrecked off Clamtown. While the absence of a precise date may not be determinable, the quest depicts how historians have fun, why they do not rest and that their work is never done.

JOHN WANAMAKER (1838–1922)

John Wanamaker, famed as one of America's greatest merchants and for the installation of one of the country's greatest pipe organs in his Philadelphia store, significantly influenced two sections of the Jersey Shore. He cofounded Sea Grove, the present Cape May Point, and later built a summer camp for employees at Island Heights, Ocean County.

Religion, a strong influence from Wanamaker's early life, motivated his first building project, the Bethany Mission Sunday School, completed in 1858 in Philadelphia. In time, it became the largest Sunday school in the country, and Wanamaker remained its superintendent for the remainder of his life. He was one of the key backers of the Sea Grove Association, a Presbyterian resort town at the southernmost point in New Jersey. His cottage, designed by James C. Sidney, who planned the community (see page 22), was one of the first built. Friends with President Benjamin Harrison, Wanamaker built a house for him there, but the president declined to accept it as he cited ethical constraints. Consequently, the house was presented to Mrs. Harrison. Thus, we understand why first ladies' finances are also scrutinized.

Wanamaker, an employer of many young people, sought to instill in them moral character, as well as provide educational opportunities. They were organized as members in the John Wanamaker Institute. In 1899, Wanamaker purchased a tract in Island Heights that overlooked Barnegat Bay, where he opened the Wanamaker Camp, a facility run with military regimens. Various starting dates for the camp have been cited, but a congressional report indicated that the 1912 encampment was its thirteenth annual. Early reveille, inspections, physical training, mess hall dining and strictly regimented life characterized vacations of the institute members. The campers did, however, enjoy swimming and sports. The camp, which continued operation past Wanamaker's death, last met in 1941 prior to an army takeover in World War II and its conversion to a Presbyterian summer camp in 1949.

George Henry White (1852-1918)

While the old adage "there are no whites living in Whitesboro" is no longer literally true, the saying reflects the founding of this section of Cape May County's Middle Township as a settlement for African Americans.

The plan to organize this separate colony for blacks was conceived by the Reverend J.H. Fishburn of Cape May around 1900, a time when a local journalist was agitating for the removal of African Americans from the Cape May resort city where so many had long served the lodging industry. The plan was for the new African American Equitable Association to establish an industrial school and sell both farms and small house lots under liberal terms to an exclusive black population.

George Henry White's embrace of the plan brought it to fruition. White, born in Bladden County, North Carolina, was the last black congressman in the post–Civil War Reconstruction era, elected from that state's so-called "Black Second" (Congressional District). He was a successful lawyer who held a number of state offices prior to winning the race for the House of Representatives in 1896. His organization advertised for and vetted settlers who possessed "good character" and "steady and industrious habits." While it was hoped that the majority of buyers would come from New Jersey, many were attracted from North Carolina and Virginia, where George White was a familiar name. Whitesboro's growth was slow but steady, and according to the town's website, "By 1909 Whitesboro boasted two churches, an industrial school, a railroad station, a post office and a hotel, all built by residents."

White left North Carolina after his second term in Congress, embittered by growing hostility to blacks, including the disenfranchisement of many as a consequence of a "grandfather clause" under an amended state constitution that barred illiterates from voting, one of the more odious of the "Jim Crow" practices. He moved to the District of Columbia and then Philadelphia. White remained active in politics but lost the bid for his party's nomination for a vacant congressional seat. He is buried in Eden Cemetery outside Philadelphia. White is remembered in his native state with roadside historical plaques in New Bern and Tarsboro.

HISTORIANS AND PRESERVATIONISTS

Derrickson W. Bennett (1930–2009)

Dery Bennett was the conscience of the Jersey Shore for decades and a tireless advocate for safeguarding the natural environment. An ardent advocate for protecting our shores, decades ago, he pointed to the futility of then existing practices. Unfortunately, little has changed while our shores continue to be assailed by overdevelopment.

Bennett, a Philadelphia native, developed a lifelong affinity for the shore by spending his youthful summers in the Avalon area. After training as a geologist and service as a navy frogman, Bennett spent his early years in education prior to a long career with the American Littoral Society, which he led as executive director from 1968 to 2003. The organization is based at Sandy Hook near some of the state's few remaining natural environments, which Bennett believed was the ideal state for shore areas. Despite personal preference for the shore's return to nature, Bennett no doubt believed that human occupancy could not be reversed, so he fought ardently to keep it under control. The society is dedicated to "encouraging the study and conservation of marine life and its habitat." Dery was in the forefront of society activism that advocated the passage of New Jersey's 1970 Wetlands Act, the 1973 Coastal Area Facility Review Act (CAFRA), the establishment of an Ocean Dumping Task Force (the forerunner of the Clean Ocean Action group, for which he served as president for twenty-five years), wider setbacks for coastal building and public access to beaches, among other accomplishments.

Derrickson Bennett was the conscience of the northern Jersey Shore for decades.

Bennett regularly assailed the practice of repeated beach replenishment by taking note of its futility as sand regularly migrates out to sea, advice infrequently followed in a culture that favors overdevelopment of our shores. Among his enduring legacy is having served as mentor to a generation of environmentalists who continue to advocate shore preservation. He is honored in his hometown with "Dery's Pond," located in the Fair Haven Fields where he loved to walk.

LEAH BLACKMAN (1817-1886)

Leah Blackman, New Jersey's first female historian, after the publication of her *History of Little Egg Harbor* in 1878, recorded the recollections gathered as a farmer's daughter and later farmer's wife. Overcoming family indifference to her desire for education and literary ambitions, she left a personal view of a half-century in her rural environs, including detail on how she attended school.

Her parents were of the Mathis family (see page 48), while she was also descended from Edward Andrews, the first settler of Tuckerton. Blackman's experience revolved around domestic farm life. Two years after the aforementioned book, Blackman, who realized that the past fifty years had created virtually a new world, began recording her memories in what would become *Leah Blackman's Old Times and Other Writings*, published in 2000 by the Tuckerton Historical Society. Much of her work revolves around domestic practices, the endless tasks of making whatever was needed, along with the growing and preservation of food. She reflected on social customs, reported the era's superstitions and recounted religious experiences. Blackman described contemporary attire and how they traveled.

The Blackman work also includes tradition that was related to her, such as early travel to the shore and Revolutionary events. She detailed "The Outlaws of the Pines." Her genealogical material was later amplified by another genealogist, June Methot, who wrote a companion volume, *Blackman Revisited*. Blackman recalled the built environment, having taken note of which structures were built before her time, while she also wrote small local histories.

Much of her material, even pieces published in newspapers, was thought to have been lost. Two boxes of her manuscripts and scrapbooks were unexpectedly given to the historical society in 1988. Their careful editing and transcription has given New Jersey this singular view of a half-century of shore life. Despite her hardships, Leah remained convinced that life on the farm was her decided preference.

MARGARET THOMAS BUCHHOLZ (B. 1933)

Manhattan native Buchholz likes to depict her Long Beach Island origins as having been brought there in 1935 in time to be evacuated for a major storm. While the event likely did not foretell future writing themes, her early *Great Storms of the Jersey Shore* is the first of a series of carefully researched, well-written and beautifully illustrated volumes that have deepened both knowledge and appreciation of the Jersey Shore and Long Beach Island.

Margaret's island family roots, which date from the Civil War era, descend through her great-grandfather John Warner Kinsey. After early education at the Barnegat Light one-room school, now a local history museum, she undertook journalism during college summers with a local summer weekly, *The Beachcomber*; this began a career that over the decades embraced varied roles including editor, reviewer and history columnist. In the 1970s, she lived off seasons in California, followed by Philadelphia, a spell that embraced extensive world travels, experiences that provided the material for summer writings.

After the 1983 death of her father, Reynold Thomas, Buchholz returned to her newly remodeled family home, located literally on the edge of Barnegat Bay in Harvey Cedars. Thomas, after the collapse of the family Wall Street business, became a commercial fisherman during the Great Depression prior to operating a dredging business, one that had to await the area's post–World War II development to flourish. He had long served the borough beginning in 1942 as a commissioner and then after 1955 as mayor.

The inspiration for the storm book, coauthored with Larry Savadove, came in the early 1990s, but publication by Down the Shore Press was delayed until 1993 as a consequence of 1992 storms, the first in January and then later the great December northeaster. The 1994 publication of *Seasons in the Sun*, a history of Harvey Cedars, established her literary territory: Long Beach Island and the Jersey Shore. Storm research led to the 1999 *Shore Chronicles*, an edited work that embraces over two centuries of travelers' accounts to the Jersey Shore.

The dangerous waters off our shores gave rise to New Jersey's designation as a "graveyard of the Atlantic." The 2004 work *New Jersey Shipwrecks* chronicles and illustrates the many maritime disasters that have plagued coastal shipping since early in the colonial era.

Two years later, *Island Album* provided a 125-year portrayal of history and life on Long Beach Island. The 330 photographs are enhanced by the text's quotations from many who experienced life here. Buchholz's oeuvre includes two family books: the reprinting of her mother's early island experiences, *Fisherman's Wife*, and *Josephine*, her World War I experiences in Washington as a munitions office worker and later career as a writer. Buchholz writes, "Islands are mythic places...an elemental world governed by the natural rhythms of sun and wind and tide." Her works illuminate one of the Jersey Shore's most storied islands and make vividly real the consequences of wind and tide when they take unnatural form.

FRANCIS PARKMAN FREEMAN (1884–1948) AND AUGUSTA HUILL SEAMAN (1879–1950)

"I am the law" was his remark that characterized the dictatorial style of legendary Jersey City mayor-boss Frank Hague, but on Island Beach, Francis Parkman Freeman was the law. His writer wife, Augusta, set many of her later children's novels at the site.

Freeman's name was initially Kenneth, but it was changed in honor of the explorer a few months after his birth in South Orange, New Jersey. Following the 1930 death of Henry Phipps, (see page 66), he would realize that his management of the latter's Jersey Shore property would involve long-term custodianship of a little-occupied, fragile environment. Phipps's stem of the island was occupied by leaseholders, popularly known as squatters, whose occupancy of their shacks was governed by Freeman, who made and enforced the rules. He was a serious amateur botanist who studied and classified the plant life on Island Beach in a scholarly manner. Island Beach was no doubt culture shock for Augusta, a New York City writer, first published in 1914, who moved there following her marriage to Frank in 1928, the year after the death of her first husband, Robert. She acclimated, relocated her only child to the island after the girl remained a year in New York and continued on the island contact with her young reader audience. Later that year, Augusta published *The Disappearance of Anne Shaw*, set in a fictionalized Island Beach. Her 1932 *The Stars of Sabra* was set on Lord Stirling's Beach, the colonial name of the island. After the American entry into World War II, the Freemans were the only remaining civilians on an Island Beach taken over by Coast Guard occupancy. Her 1942 *The Case of the Calico Crab* addressed the real threat of Nazi saboteurs.

The two became a power couple before the term was coined. Property taxes on Phipps's estate were collected by the three mainland townships to which the long stretch of beach belonged. The municipality law as it then existed made it relatively simple to incorporate a borough given political cooperation. After Freeman was able to secure the incorporation of the Borough of Island Beach in 1933, he, Augusta and a retired Coast Guard captain ran the municipality. Frank was mayor, while his wife was borough clerk and tax collector. Of course, property taxes stayed on the island. Since a separate municipality became redundant after the State of New Jersey acquired the property, the borough was dissolved in 1965 with the territory then being made part of Berkeley Township.

J. Louise Jost (1910–1999)

In her long career as an educator, Miss Jost, as she was known, instilled an appreciation of history in legions of fourth graders, founded a historical museum and oversaw virtually the entirety of historical life in the ancient, venerable Borough of Shrewsbury.

A native of Bayonne, Jost taught third grade in 1953–54 and then in the following year moved to the fourth grade, the academic year for instruction in New Jersey history. She organized the Jerseyana Club for afterschool historical activities, naming the group for Henry Charlton Beck's widely followed Jerseyana newspaper column. Awareness in 1961 of the forthcoming 1964 New Jersey Tercentenary led the children to undertake an ambitious art project: the research, design and fabrication of a New Jersey history–themed mosaic. After completion in the unexpectedly short spell of one year, they deemed the skillful work as the first gift to New Jersey for that celebrated anniversary. Among other projects, Jost guided the students to complete the substantial publications, *Shrewsbury Century Homes* and *Historical Shrewsbury*, works that are still utilized.

Jost became co-chair of the Shrewsbury Association for the Restoration of the Allen House, popularly known as SARAH, a group successful in that purpose and one that led to the formation of the Shrewsbury Historical Society, organized in 1972 and incorporated the following year. A lack of school leadership following her 1971 retirement led to the waning of the Jerseyana Club, which turned its collections over to the new society.

One of Jost's greatest accomplishments followed the 1976 destruction by fire of a carriage house on borough hall property. Starting with a borough grant and modest insurance proceeds, she led a successful fundraising campaign for the construction of their museum, which opened in 1982. Many awards honored Jost and the organizations she led, including recognition from the New Jersey Historical Commission, the League of Historical Societies of New Jersey and Zonta of Monmouth County, which designated her 1982 Woman of the Year. Her greatest pride was her students, many of whom later visited or served the historical society, where they often expressed fondness for their fourth-grade memories and teacher. Some who never knew Jost in school and wondered what the experience

The fourth grade never left J. Louise Jost's endearing personality, it, at times emerging in her interactions with visitors.

was like received hints, as she never lost the bearing and mien of an elementary school teacher.

She claimed her burial place at the front of Christ Church Cemetery located opposite the museum was chosen to permit her to oversee the museum from the hereafter. Many who knew her believed she was not joking.

John Bailey Lloyd (1932–2003)

Although Lloyd was born in Johnstown, Pennsylvania, he was so deeply immersed in Long Beach Island history that many thought him to be a native. His origins on the island dated to 1942, when he began visiting North Beach with his family. In time, he served here as a lifeguard.

John studied English, and after employment with a publisher and work as a stockbroker, he became a librarian as a second career, which followed permanent settlement in Beach Haven in 1977. His historical writings, which he began as a columnist for the two island newspapers, developed a wide readership after his articles were inserted in the full-page advertisements of Bay State Bank. Interest in a permanent format led to his first book in 1986, *Eighteen Miles of History*, issued as a slender paperback.

At that time, John thought that this publication was a thorough recounting of the island's past, but he had only begun to uncover Long Beach's rich history. Adding to his early childhood experiences, which began according to his friend and publisher Ray Fisk at a point when "he arrived…in time to see old landmarks like the Beach Haven boardwalk, the Engleside Hotel and the vast emptiness of the Island as it once was," John absorbed the memories of the old-timers and gathered their pictures. This led to two more major works and an expansion of the first. *Six Miles at Sea*, a 176-page hardcover volume followed in 1990, three years prior to the comparably sized republication of *Eighteen Miles of History*.

John's employment with the Ocean County Library provided ready access to historical resources, which he continued to mine. A natural storyteller, he engaged audiences at the Long Beach Island Museum, Beach Haven, and in a wide circle of venues, taking pleasure in recreating the atmosphere of past eras.

John's final work, *Two Centuries of History on Long Beach Island*, substantially complete at his untimely death, was published posthumously in 2005 after editing. John observed that all who came to Long Beach Island, excepting the shipwrecked, "came out of pure enjoyment and returned year after year for the same reason." His compelling books provide similar pleasure as well as insight. They keep readers returning for an inimitable in-print Long Beach Island experience.

Reverend Carl McIntire (1906–2002)

Many controversies enveloped the life of the Reverend McIntire, which make an objective evaluation of his career difficult, including his role of accidental preservationist.

Born in Michigan to a Presbyterian minister father and raised in Oklahoma, the son began his religious education at Princeton Theological Seminary but after two years switched to the new fundamentalist Westminster Theological Seminary. McIntire became a flash point, standing that grew out of his militant opposition to mainline churches, anti-Communist zealotry, pro-war activism and ownership of a marginal Bible school. Attracted to the city by post-1962 storm real estate bargains, he arrived in Cape May in 1963 with the purchase of the Admiral Hotel, planned as headquarters of his Christian conference center and Shelton College.

When preservation of Cape May's Victorian-era built environment was still at the crossroads, McIntire bought a number of threatened buildings, which he typically moved for use with the conference-Bible facility. Maintenance was often questionable, while he failed to pay taxes, as he claimed exemptions for which he did not qualify. After Shelton, which was not accredited, was barred in New Jersey from granting degrees, McIntire moved to Florida, although he later returned to Cape May.

The Reverend McIntire became a broadcast evangelist prior to the famed media names, but a dispute with the Federal Communications Commission over the fairness doctrine resulted in a loss of his radio station's license. Barred from broadcasting from the roof of his renamed Christian Admiral Hotel, McIntire purchased a World War II minesweeper and then made a short-lived attempt to broadcast off Cape May from beyond the then three-mile territorial limit. Redbaiting politics during the specter of the McCarthy era fueled controversy that grew from his attacks on other churches.

Some McIntire buildings deteriorated from deferred maintenance. Once the city's largest property owners, his failure to pay taxes resulted in an approximately $500,000 indebtedness to Cape May at the time of his declared bankruptcy; his holdings dissolved. An evaluation depends on whether McIntire is credited for his initial rescue of buildings or condemned for poor custodianship as an opportunistic preservationist.

GEORGE H. MOSS JR. (1923–2009)

George Moss combined his business career with a passion for collecting and a penchant for writing. He produced some of New Jersey's finest illustrated books.

Born in New York, but proud to claim he was the fourth generation on the Jersey Shore, George served in the Office of Strategic Services in the Middle East and Italy during World War II prior to work on Wall Street, which led to membership in the New York Stock Exchange, early retirement and the opportunity to focus on the preservation of Monmouth County history. Foremost among his many collecting interests were photographs and documents, which prompted George to call himself "a paper archaeologist." George's specialty, the shore from Sandy Hook to Long Branch, was largely embraced by his first book in 1964, *Nauvoo to the Hook—An Iconography of a Barrier Beach*, followed two years later by *Steamboat to the Shore*. He organized the Ploughshare Press in order to control every aspect of production, including paper stock and typeface. George founded the museum at Sandy Hook.

A collector with many interests, George Moss focused on preserving Monmouth County history.

George's first photographic volume was the 1971 *Double Exposure—Early Stereographic Views of Historic Monmouth County*. Both *Nauvoo* and *Double Exposure* were reissued years later in revised editions. Two subsequent Jersey Shore works were coauthored with Karen L. Schnitzspahn, the 1993 *Those Innocent Years—Images of the Jersey Shore from the Pach*

Photographic Collection and the 2000 *Victorian Summers at the Grand Hotels of Long Branch New Jersey.*

George wrote many articles, including a year-long series for the nation's bicentennial, and shorter works including booklets on Sea Bright and Holy Cross Church, Rumson. In 2002, the bicentennial pieces were reprinted in hardcover as *Twice Told Tales.* His educational works included *Monmouth—Our Indian Heritage* and two portfolios of documents, intended to give students experience with primary sources.

George served many organizations and his community, the former including the Monmouth County Historical Association as a trustee for many years, and the latter as long-term president of the Rumson Borough Council. He was the officially appointed historian of Monmouth County from 1999 through 2008 and took satisfaction assisting other authors and historians. His numerous honors included in 1998 the Richard J. Hughes Award from the New Jersey Historical Commission, history's highest honor in the state.

The Jersey Shore was enriched not only by George's remarkable body of work but also by his warmth, good nature and willingness to share.

FRED WINSLOW NOYES JR. (1905–1987) AND ETHEL LINGELBACH NOYES (1911–1979)

Fred, a Philadelphia native and academically trained artist, and Ethel, a folklorist/antiquarian, claim two major accomplishments that enrich South Jersey life. After they assembled and preserved the Historic Towne of Smithville, they established the Noyes Museum of Art.

While they knew one another in their earlier years in rural South Jersey, their different backgrounds did not appear to have the makings of a love match. However, Fred and Ethel's relationship jelled during his convalescence following his return from the war with serious battle wounds. It is claimed that her intervention prevented the amputation of Fred's leg. They married in 1945, shortly prior to his army discharge. As Fred continued his lifelong passion of painting, they opened an antiques business, which they first operated in their Absecon home prior to relocation on Route 30. Fred also gave art lessons, restored furniture and pursued a second passion, decoy collecting. In 1951, they found on Old New York Road, or Route 9, in Smithville a deteriorating former inn that dated from the latter eighteenth century. They bought the place, restored it and then opened the Smithville Inn, a lunch and tearoom with antique shop, a venture that would change the region's history and underscore their different personal make-ups.

The large tract owned by the Noyeses permitted them to fulfill Ethel's ambition to preserve South Jersey history and promote its understanding. They acquired buildings for relocation to the inn's grounds. While initially the two managed the operation's every aspect, the business grew as the Historic Towne of Smithville emerged and what became a full-service restaurant flourished. Their distinct personalities are suggested by the title of Judith Courter's fine, in-depth study, *Fred and Ethel Noyes of Smithville, New Jersey—The Artist and the Entrepreneur*. He was a jovial, more relaxed creative type while she was a driven businesswoman. Ethel envisioned and planned every detail, while Fred tended to reserve himself for the big decisions. While he was fond of the ladies, their relationship endured and worked.

The Village, which initially combined a section of exhibition artisans and shops, became a tourist attraction. As their staff grew, Ethel attempted to micromanage employees' lives, preferring they not socialize if it would mar readiness for the next day's work. Active in South Jersey business circles, Ethel was honored with awards and recognition.

Finances were never secure, even after Historic Smithville's public stock sale in 1972. When American Broadcasting Company bought the operation, including 2,200 acres in 1974 for a reported $7,000,000, they also assumed $2,000,000 in liabilities. Fred and Ethel stayed on as hosts.

Plump, diabetic Fred had the medical problem that bore Ethel's scrutiny, but she long had a heart condition that took her life, an unexpected passing that delayed plans to establish an art museum. The Noyes Museum of Art opened in 1983. Fred, whose art and decoys formed the core of the museum's collection, remained active there until his death. The museum thrives in affiliation with Richard Stockton State College.

HENRY PHIPPS (1839-1930)

Henry Phipps is listed with the preservationists, but it is unlikely placement. His former Jersey Shore estate forms Island Beach State Park, a rare and spectacular natural seashore landscape, but Phipps actually intended to build a high-class development. His plans, however, were thwarted by the dual inconveniences of the Great Depression and death. Phipps possesses a worthy and lengthy record of philanthropy.

Born in Philadelphia, Phipps was raised in western Pennsylvania, where modest career beginnings included work as a messenger and office boy. Hired by Andrew Carnegie, he earned a partnership after he demonstrated his mettle by skill in raising capital. Phipps was able to build great wealth through the rise of the steel industry but also through shrewd real estate investments.

Phipps's early public benefactions included in 1885 a conservatory in a park in Allegheny, Pennsylvania, then his home, followed in 1893 by the conservatory in Schenley Park, Pittsburg. He funded an agricultural college in India and sent recovery money to South Africa after the Boer War. Phipps's generous donations to medical causes included funds for a psychiatric clinic at Johns Hopkins and the Phipps Institute at the University of Pennsylvania for Tuberculosis Research. Phipps built a Fifth Avenue mansion after moving to New York around 1900, but he also gave $1,000,000 for the erection of model tenements in the city. The family also had a suburban estate in Great Neck, Long Island.

Island Beach, a nearly ten-mile strip of barrier beach north of Barnegat Inlet, was considered for public use for some years prior to Governor A. Harry Moore's veto in 1926 of a bill for the State of New Jersey to acquire the land. Apparently, neither had the state the inclination to find the funds nor the governor the vision for future recreational needs. Phipps, whose major real estate investments included a major part of Palm Beach, Florida, bought the property that August with intentions to develop; only three structures were built.

Following Phipps's death, the tract was maintained by his estate, a fascinating story beyond the scope of this profile, but see Frank Freeman, page 59. The state acquired the property in 1953, land that is now one of the Atlantic's most revered preserved natural environments.

CAROLYN PITTS (1924-2008)

Carolyn Pitts saved Cape May. Others were involved, of course, and some had to be dragged reluctantly into the real world of preservation, but Pitts was the single person most responsible for preserving the city's Victorian-era built environment, including the many architectural gems that have earned the city's historic district National Historic Landmark stature.

Mary Carolyn Pitts, known as Carolyn and raised in Pennsylvania, began her career as an art school instructor in the Philadelphia Museum of Art after earning a masters in fine arts at the University of Pennsylvania. Later a Fulbright Scholar who lectured in Europe, she started work with the National Park Service as an architectural historian at least by 1962 when she went to Cape May in March to survey damage by the horrific Ash Wednesday Northeaster. That storm was the signal event to begin the transformation of a faded, then overlooked resort into a tourist magnet. The campaign that resulted in the triumph of history and preservation was neither short nor easy.

An infusion of post-storm federal urban renewal funds prompted the local renascence. While history was widely regarded as a key asset, some officials would have used history to remove rather than preserve. As one example, they offered the modern creation of the Washington Street Mall. Miss Pitts, as she was generally called, insisted on authenticity and provided the scholarship to reinforce her case. She obtained grants to hire architects and historians to uncover forgotten architectural history. She had been called brassy, bold, contentious and impatient, just the qualities needed for dogged opposition to those who would destroy, a force that included a sitting mayor and owners seeking easy solutions. Pitts and three coauthors published the *Cape May Handbook*, a book acclaimed nationally as a model guide. Pitts's public motivation is summed up in her remark, "If we can get people to read a plaque on a building and just take a good look at the building, then we've moved a step past the throwaway society we have become."

At the National Park Service, she conducted studies for over 25 percent of the then 2,200 National Historic Landmark sites, a designation that comprises an honor roll of the National Register of Historic Places. Her preservation work was honored in 1991 with the Meritorious Service Award.

JOSEPH E. AND PATRICIA ANNE SALVATORE

The assembly and opening to the public of Cold Spring Village is a restoration for the ages, but the Salvatores undertook two massive projects. The second, at the former Naval Air Station Wildwood, is now an aviation museum. The two sites, among Cape May County's most significant places, stand as monuments to the Salvatores' vision and work ethic.

When Joe, a Wildwood native, and Anne, now retired medical professionals, he an orthopedic surgeon and she a nurse, sought a summer home in 1969, one was available with thirty-five acres and the former Cold Spring Grange No. 132. After its acquisition, they later found the threatened old Marshalltown School, which they moved to their property. This project brought newspaper publicity and the offer of other buildings, notably the Dennisville Inn, also relocated to the site. The accumulation of redundant, antique buildings took a life of its own as the Salvatores became dismayed with the thought that anything old would be demolished. Regular visitors to Colonial Williamsburg and Old Sturbridge Village, the idea of a restored village took form. The family went through a spell when they scoured the Cape May countryside in searches for artifacts for the village. After considerable research, their Cold Spring Village opened to the public in 1981.

The village was initially maintained personally by the Salvatores, but as the venture and number of employees grew, public stewardship was sought. Thus, the village was given to the County of Cape May in 1984. While public entities can operate historic sites, Cape May had other thoughts and in 1993 returned the site to the Salvatores, who then organized foundation ownership. The Historic Cold Spring Village Foundation was formed to operate the village, today an open-air living history museum of twenty-six buildings. Anne has been its unpaid executive director and guiding light since day one. Her accomplishments were recognized by the New Jersey Historical Commission with the 2010 presentation of the Richard J. Hughes Award, history's highest honor in the state of New Jersey.

Joe, who needed a project in 1995 after retiring, unexpectedly learned that the dilapidated Hangar No. 1 of the Naval Air Station Wildwood was threatened with destruction. From his youth he recalled the place as a constant hub of activity, loved airplanes and by nature enjoys tackling big jobs and keeping busy. The building became available for a token one dollar, along with the willingness to undertake an enormous restoration project, 92,000 square feet of pigeon-infested barrenness with about half of its 4,400 windows broken. Joe had the ability to marshal forces for the restoration and the foresight to perceive a museum.

The Naval Air Station Wildwood, a World War II training facility for dive-bomber pilots commissioned on April 1, 1943, was busy with an enormous number of takeoffs and landings; they peaked at 16,994 during October 1944. Inevitable accidents took a toll of forty-two known killed in 129 crashes. The station became surplus after the war with the result that many buildings were sold and removed from the site. The airfield, which went through a number of incarnations, is now Cape May County Airport.

The museum, operated by the Naval Air Station Wildwood Foundation, cofounded in 1995 by Joe, who serves as unpaid executive director, is dedicated as a memorial to the aviators who perished there. The numerous and varied exhibits center around the museum's collection of aircraft, which numbers twenty-six and is growing. Of special Jersey Shore interest is the Coast Guard Area, recognition of a branch of the military that is crucial to the rescue of mariners as well as downed aviators. Other exhibits and facilities evolve and expand.

Cape May County, widely known for its beach resorts, also possesses a rich and deep history that extends beyond the shore. Two of its gems exist from the dedication of one couple, Joe and Anne Salvatore.

MARITIME

JAMES P. ALLAIRE (1785–1858)

James P. Allaire's identity on the Jersey Shore is generally associated with his iron-producing Howell Works, but history should not overlook his significance in maritime annals. Locally, he operated a line of steamships and was a significant shipper from a once prominent but now forgotten port. In addition, an Allaire vessel was involved in one of the country's most tragic wrecks, and in New York, Allaire was a major manufacturer of steam engines.

Apparently born in Nova Scotia where his loyalist, Huguenot family had fled after the Revolution, Allaire established himself in the brass business, had a foundry in lower Manhattan and built a relationship with Robert Fulton after he fabricated the brass works for Fulton's pioneer steamship *Clermont*. Following the latter's death and a short-lived partnership, Allaire took over Fulton's works in Jersey City and moved them to New York, where he built a leading business for marine engines. Allaire extended his maritime interests to ship ownership.

Allaire was attracted to Monmouth County by Benjamin Howell in order to secure a source of iron. He bought his Howell Works in 1822 to obtain its considerable supply of bog iron. The isolated location in the Pinelands required a village to house workers and support operations. Along with inland transport to reach the water, Allaire established shipping operations at Eatontown Dock (now Oceanport) on the Shrewsbury River; he also sailed his steamers out of Red Bank on the Navesink River.

Allaire also maintained oceangoing operations, at times taking interests in ships for which he supplied engines. Great risk accompanied the business, both for mariners and owners. The new *Home*, one of the finest of the Allaire vessels, after sailing from New York for Charleston on October 7, 1837, was battered by storms off Hatteras, North Carolina. After the doomed ship was run aground north of Ocracoke in an attempt to preserve life, it broke up about a quarter of a mile from shore. About seventy of ninety passengers and twenty-five of the crew of forty-five lost their lives. The loss had a dismal impact on the financial market, which at the time was also shaken by the Panic of 1837. Allaire's finances suffered even greater damage by the discovery of means to refine iron ore, a process that killed the bog iron business. His fortune depleted, Allaire left New York for his Howell residence in a village that for practical purposes became abandoned until its revival in the third quarter of the twentieth century as Allaire State Park.

Amos Birdsall (1829–1909)

Captain Birdsall became a premier example of how an ambitious seaman could elevate himself to maritime owner prior to becoming a successful businessman.

Amos, born in Waretown to a family that immigrated to Long Island in the seventeenth century prior to relocation in the Egg Harbor environs during the eighteenth, went to sea at age twelve. By sixteen he was mate of the *Amos Birdsall*, apparently named for his grandfather, and by eighteen was a master who sailed the schooner *Eliza Hamilton* out of Barnegat Inlet to New York. Continuing his seamanship as master, Amos extended his voyages to Virginia, the West Indies and the Gulf of Mexico. When at twenty-three he built the large schooner *Jacob Birdsall* at Waretown, Amos was quarter owner, master and manager.

Amos, who sailed until his middle years, became increasingly active as ship builder and owner, typically in conjunction with his sons. After relocation to Toms River, Birdsall built a substantial house on Washington Street and joined the First National Bank of Toms River. After he became its second president, he served in that office for about fifteen years until his death, his career reported in the January 6, 1910 *New Jersey Courier*. His descendent Jack Birdsall donated the 26 Hadley Avenue property to the Ocean County Historical Society; a room in their museum at this location honors the Birdsalls.

Captain Thomas Bond (1799-1891)

Thomas Bond's long career on Long Beach Island bridged the earliest efforts of rescue at sea to a professional lifesaving service. Present when the island was accessible only by boat, he saw Long Beach later thrive as a railroad resort.

Bond, a watchcase maker in New York (in 1846, located at 41 Ann Street), bought Philadelphia House in 1851, eager to engage in recreational gunning. The place, renamed Long Beach House, attracted other sportsmen. The pre-lifesaving service facility, erected nearby, was called a house of refuge, but its inadequacy, typical of the volunteer era, often required Bond to provide sustenance. After the *Georgia* wrecked in 1847, all four hundred passengers were saved, but their care was left to Bond. He sued to recover his enormous outlay, but a judgment against an insolvent ship owner still burdened Bond with the expense. After the paid lifesaving service was established, Bond was appointed lifesaver.

Thomas Bond is a legend on Long Beach Island, as an early hotel keeper and lifesaver. *Courtesy of Ocean County Historical Society.*

Competition from more commodious hotels that were built following the railroad's arrival on Long Beach constrained Bond's precarious finances in his later years. James Holgate's several land purchases from Bond resulted in renaming the southern island Holgate instead of Bond's. His reputation as congenial host and public-minded citizen brought him legendary stature.

JOHN MAXSON BROWN (1808-1896)

Early in our maritime history, the shipwrecked had no lifesaving service, no crew of lifesavers on shore eager to render rescue and no house of refuge if good fortune landed him or her on shore. Their only hope depended on the rare resident who would volunteer aid, such as John Maxson Brown.

Brown was born into a maritime family, to a father, William, who was a prominent boat builder on the Manasquan River, a location in present Brielle. After Brown went to sea around 1829, he soon became the master of vessels but spent much of his career on the Squan Beach waterfront. "During the Mexican War he commanded a transport in the Gulf, and with his crew he was enrolled for service on shore at Brazos, his crew afterwards receiving bounty for that service," according to Woolman and Rose, one of the better among the few sources on Brown. From the shore, he engaged in the wrecking business, often in the employ of the Coast Wrecking Company, which, its name notwithstanding, is in the service of saving vessels and cargo for owners and/or insurance underwriters. Brown's legendary lifesaving exploits began, as was noted, prior to the establishment of the Life Saving Service, but following its organization, he was placed in charge of a number of stations. The gold-plated medal awarded for those services in 1857 specified his actions on the notable *Cornelius Grinnell* and *New Era* wrecks.

Brown was married to Mary Pearce in 1830; two of their sons were lost at sea. He is credited with saving hundreds of passengers and crew, perhaps a greater number than any other lifesaver. After he retired in 1873, his home was made into the Union House, a hotel on the river at Union Lane Brielle. The place was treated as a pilgrimage site and visited by many whom he had saved.

JOHN LOTT DORSETT (1830-1910)

John Lott Dorsett, a lifelong man of the sea, was another pre–Life Saving Service volunteer rescuer, but one who also chronicled the maritime disasters in his Squan Beach section of the shore. He was also a bibliophile but may be best remembered for making an unusual, even bizarre, maritime artifact. Dorsett built a cabinet assembled from the woods of twenty-five wrecks.

Born in an old family homestead near the headwaters of Barnegat Bay, Dorsett became a ship joiner while an adolescent. He subsequently went to sea, learned marine architecture and became well known as a builder of light-draught craft for the inland coastal waters of the Atlantic. Dorsett was legendary for his rescue efforts:

> *Long before the U.S. government took over the Volunteer Life Saving Service on the coast, Captain Dorsett dwelt on Squan Beach on the present site of Mantoloking and with a crew as indomitable as himself, succored hundreds of lives and millions in marine property on the long stretch of then desolate beach between Barnegat and Manasquan inlets, without reward, shelter or sustenance, in those days and nights of prolific shipwreck.*

He was later a keeper in the era of the organized volunteer service. Dorsett kept a record of maritime disasters on the stem of shore from Barnegat Inlet to Ocean Grove, a valued resource to insurance underwriters, ship- and cargo owners, as well as relatives of drowned or injured seamen.

Dorsett in his later years was builder and owner of a forty-six-foot-long schooner, initially named for him but later renamed *Rosamond*, on which he carried sporting passengers. The vessel offered "spring beds and clean linen" and was "supplied with the best food the market affords," according to his advertisement, which modestly claimed, "Her record is established."

The prize of a book collection noteworthy in its times was a seventeenth-century Dutch-printed Bible. The aforementioned cabinet was in its time a well-known, albeit ghastly, curio. The woods from the twenty-five identified wrecks included pieces from some of the best-known period disasters, including the *Powhattan*, *Ayrshire* and *New Era*.

In 1849, Captain Dorsett married Margaret Ann Chapman of Freehold, who predeceased him in 1878. He was survived by two sons and a daughter. The best source of information was his friend Frank McConnell, who recounted his memories in his *Monmouth Democrat* columns on May 14, 1908, and June 30, 1910, the latter ten days after Dorsett's death and the source of the previous quotation.

JOSEPH FRANCIS (1801–1893)

Francis, an innovator and inventor with small watercraft, began building boats as a youth. His greatest creation, the lifecar, made him a vitally important figure in maritime rescue.

Born in Boston, Francis placed first in a boat-building competition at age twelve. A manufacturer of various craft, his greatest conception was iron for constructing a lifecar, a small, enclosed boat looking not unlike a submarine. After a rope line was shot to a distressed vessel, the lifecar was sent on the line to the ship where passengers huddled inside to return to shore. Traveling inside was likely as terrifying as it was effective. Its first test was the January 12, 1850 wreck of the *Ayrshire* off Squan Beach. The crew and all but 1 of the 166 passengers were saved through repeated trips by Francis's device. The only fatality was a panicked man, swept away after leaping atop the car. While grateful over his invention's success, Francis was disappointed over the lack of federal government support and dismayed over failure to recognize his contributions. Francis's travels to Europe brought him honors and acceptance of his numerous devices.

American recognition was late but significant. In 1890, Congress honored him with a large gold medal, ceremoniously presented by President Harrison. Recounting the event in a letter to friend Thomas Bond in the collection of the Ocean County Historical Society dated April 21, 1890,

Joseph Francis's invention of the metal lifecar is one of the most important lifesaving appliances ever created. *Collection of Ocean City Historical Society.*

Francis was emphatic in claiming that the recognition would "establish the fact irrevocably that I am the founder and originator of the Life Saving Service in 1812 and appliances from that time to 1850 and for all time to come." Thus, he asserted that his inventions rather than the government's building stations were the real origin of lifesaving in America.

Francis settled in Toms River, where his fine home on the water was adapted as the Riverview Hotel, long a popular meeting-dining venue for local groups until destruction by fire on December 25, 1965.

CHARLES E. HANKINS (1925-2003)

Hankins's long career took him from a builder of a traditional Jersey Shore boat type to recognition as a craft-cultural icon. When he retired, an era was over as his cherished wood Sea Bright skiff had been supplanted by fiberglass.

Hankins's father, Charles M., began the Lavallette boat building business in 1912 following employment with another noted boat builder. After the son Charles built his first boat as a teen, he spent the World War II years with the Coast Guard and then after the war resumed work full time. Their specialty boat, made for use on the New Jersey ocean shore, was designed for its ability to be launched directly from the beach into active surf. While many boats with overlapping planks are designated sea skiffs, the local variety, named for the town on the northern shore, is only about three-feet deep, can float in a mere eight inches of water and has a slanting stern that enables water, while the craft is being beached, to flow under, rather than into the boat.

Hawkins, whose output numbered upward of four thousand boats, built them in various sizes depending on use, but typically sixteen or eighteen feet. Pound fishermen required longer thirty-three-foot boats. Lifesavers liked the skiffs for their maneuverability. Rumrunners preferred twenty-eight footers, which they equipped with powerful engines for speed.

In 1993, the National Endowment for the Arts designated Charles as a National Heritage Fellow as recognition that his skilled boat building was an art; the award came with a $10,000 fellowship. He traveled to Washington, where be built a boat on the National Mall for the illumination and education of thousands. His work was also then featured in a film, *The Sea Bright Skiff: Working on the Jersey Shore*. At Hankins's retirement seven years later, he had no regrets. After a satisfying life's work, he realized the era was over, his

BIRTH OF THE JERSEY SHORE

esteemed wood craft replaced by the fiberglass he disdained. A small park on Barnegat Bay honors the family, including his wife, Anna, who served Lavallette for many years as borough clerk.

CAPTAIN GEORGE H. HILDRETH (1822-1897)

The varied career of Hildreth began in the maritime trades, and he ended as one of the richest men in Cape May, but a romantic entanglement intervened.

Born in Rio Grande, Cape May County, to a significant, long-established family, after Hildreth went to sea at age sixteen, his early maritime ventures, as reported in Woolman and Rose, read as a litany of lost ships. He later became partial owner of one or more vessels and joined wrecking crews, no doubt believing that salvage was preferable to being rescued. In 1870, Hildreth became keeper of Life-Saving Station No. 39 in Cape May.

Having had experience with wayward waters, in 1847, Hildreth built the Columbia House in "the Meadow" at Cape May, a risky venture in that tide-threatened swamp. However, his success led to its profitable sale and subsequent investment in agricultural real estate, milling, other hotels and fish oil processing.

Hildreth married in 1850 but apparently lost his first wife. While it is known that he was survived by a widow and six children, prior to his remarriage, he courted Sophia Cahill, the wealthy widow of Thomas E. Cahill, the former president of the Knickerbocker Ice Company. She lost interest in him over time, presuming she once had any. Hildreth believed otherwise, so he sued her in 1882 for breach of promise of marriage with the claim he made $2,000 of housing improvements to accommodate her. What he did build in 1882 was the Carroll Villa Hotel. He withdrew the case in 1884. Even then, the newspapers dwelled on this type of story, including the December 15, 1882 and January 23, 1884 issues of the *Philadelphia Inquirer*.

CAPTAIN CHARLES P. IRWIN (1867-1951)

Captain Irwin, son of a mariner, plied the water, built boats and founded what is arguably the oldest family-owned marina in America. He was at the focal point of every aspect of early maritime activity in his native Red Bank, where he spent his entire life.

78

In 1884, the captain opened his boat operation on the Navesink east of Wharf Avenue on what had been known as "the Green," a stem of the riverfront that in former days had been treated as virtually public property. He began performing miscellaneous work in a 5- by 5-foot shack that he rented annually for a dozen soft shell crabs, which was soon supplemented by a suitable building. In 1909, Captain Irwin designed and helped build a major expansion, a 32- by 198-foot concrete block structure with a 32-foot ell. He also built bulkheads along the river. Owner of a master pilot's license since 1892, one of his routes was a passenger run between Red Bank and Highlands.

Captain Irwin built and raced motor and ice yachts, including the famed A-Class iceboats *Georgie* and *Georgie II*, built in 1885 and 1902 respectively.

Captain Charles Irwin, proud of many maritime accomplishments, was an unbeatable iceboat racer. *Courtesy of Glenn Vogel.*

In 1949, the eighty-one-year-old racer claimed that he was undefeated in the latter and, as was reported in the February 12, 1949 *New York Times*, he repeated his longstanding challenge to the iceboating world to try. He helped organize the Red Bank Boat Races, which evolved into the once widely followed National Sweepstakes Regatta. The captain, who served on the Red Bank Borough Council, had three sons, including Edwin, who continued the Red Bank operation. Charles Jr. operated a marina in Florida, while Joseph, after he entered politics, served for decades on the Monmouth County Board of Chosen Freeholders. The Red Bank yard, now Irwin Marine, is operated by the captain's grandson Channing. The captain was one of his town's best-known and widely respected figures.

CAPTAIN JOHN JEFFRIES (1829-1887)

No ordinary marker, Captain John Jeffries's monument is on the National Register of Historic Places.

The life of Jeffries of the long-established Atlantic County pioneer maritime family may not have risen above his hardworking contemporaries, but in death, he became a symbol for the Great Egg Harbor maritime community.

Jeffries was born at English Creek to a family that had been in the area by 1775, one no doubt the patronym for Jeffers or Jeffries Landing, a place known to have been in existence as Great Egg Harbor Landing by 1775. Great Egg Harbor ports were shipbuilding sites since at least the third quarter of the eighteenth century. One yard, operated by Captain Samuel Gaskill, built in 1872 the three-masted schooner

Twenty-one Friends for Jeffries, a vessel financed by and named for twenty-one Philadelphia Quakers.

In 1885, the *Twenty-one Friends*, carrying a load of lumber from Brunswick, Georgia, collided with the schooner *John D. May* off Hatteras and sustained damage that justified to its Captain Barrett the abandonment of the ship. The crew was rescued, but unexpectedly, the sturdy ship did not sink. The unmanned *Twenty-one Friends* drifted about the Atlantic for about two years prior to coming ashore in Ireland. There, the cargo was salvaged, while locals returned the ship into service as a fishing vessel.

The significance of the *Twenty-one Friends*, a story well known in "ghost ship" annals, is reflected on Jeffries's grave marker. His monument at the Scullville Bible Church Cemetery (formerly Palestine Bible Protestant Church), the most prominent in the yard, was listed on the National Register of Historic Places in 1984, as "it addresses two related industries, the people who caused them to prosper and the calamities which could alter their intertwined lives." The register application recounts the Jeffries history.

GENERAL GEORGE GORDON MEADE (1815-1872)

While Meade's fame rests with his Civil War command of the Army of the Potomac, he was a civil engineer before he began the second phase of his military career. He is credited with the design of several lighthouses, beginning with work on the Delaware Bay. Barnegat, perhaps his most notable project, followed his Absecon Lighthouse. Meade also designed lighthouses in Florida but apparently not Cape May, for which he is at times given credit, although he did help supervise construction.

Born in Spain to a Philadelphia merchant who was then serving as a United States naval agent, Meade graduated from West Point with the class of 1835 and fought the Seminole Indians in Florida, prior to resigning his commission to pursue an engineering career. In 1842, he rejoined the army in the Corps of Engineers.

Barnegat Inlet, among the most treacherous of Jersey Coastal water, eroded the ground around the original 1835 lighthouse, which necessitated its move while a replacement was built. Meade's design, half painted in red, the other white and first lit in 1859, has become one of the most iconic symbols of the Jersey Shore.

General George G. Meade, famed as a Civil War hero, built lighthouses on the Jersey Shore.

Meade, appointed a brigadier general in August 1861, saw action in most of the eastern campaigns of the war but was surprised when he was appointed commander of the Army of the Potomac early in the Gettysburg campaign. Assuming leadership under trying circumstances, Meade's tactics, notably his force's defense of Lee's assault, contributed greatly to the Union victory.

Meade, who remained in the army, died from complications of old war wounds. A number of monuments honor his memory, along with the naming of Fort Meade in Maryland. The General Meade Society of Philadelphia meets annually to commemorate his November 6 passing.

WILLIAM A. NEWELL (1817–1901)

Newell's greater career was spent in public office and as a medical doctor, but he is endeared at the Jersey Shore as the father of the United States Life Saving Service, a claim also made by Joseph Francis (see page 75). Born in Ohio during his New Jersey parents' short-term venture in the Midwest, Newell was educated in New Brunswick and trained as a physician at the University of Pennsylvania. During his early practice at Manahawkin, Newell was a helpless witness to a maritime disaster, the loss of all on board the Austrian brig *Terasto* in 1839. This experience motivated Newell to seek funding for an organized rescue service. After Newell bought a house in Allentown in western Monmouth County in 1844, he was elected as a Whig to the House of Representatives in 1846 and reelected in 1848. He accomplished what he considered his signature career achievement by securing in 1848 a modest $10,000 congressional appropriation as an addition to a lighthouse bill. In the recent past, historians

Dr. William Newell's long career took him many places in multiple roles; for the shore he secured a lifesaving appropriation. *Photograph by Matthew Brady; courtesy of Monmouth County Archives.*

have called this bill the "Newell Act," but there is no evidence of such a named law. This accomplishment, although quite significant, was more political maneuvering than authorship of legislation. Securing such a service was a hard sell, as exemplified by a similar appropriation attained in 1847 by Congressman Robert McClelland of Michigan that remained unspent.

Newell was narrowly elected governor in 1856 as a candidate of both the American and the new Republican Parties, which jointly sought to defeat the dominant Democrats. He was not an activist in the office and, in brief, became enmeshed in nativist politics. In 1861, President Lincoln appointed him the superintendent of the Life Saving Service in New Jersey, an office he held until rejoining the House in 1865 for a single term. Failing at future attempts for elective office, Newell was appointed by President Hayes in 1880 as governor of the Territory of Washington, a position he held until 1884, prior to one year as United States Indian Inspector for the northwest. Newell practiced medicine in Olympia for fourteen years prior to his return to Allentown in 1899.

PRESIDENTS

Ulysses S. Grant (1822–1885)

Grant's stature as the quintessential Jersey Shore presidential visitor stems from his ownership of two Long Branch houses and his long residence there, but also from his mingling with the people in his environs and the extensive following he drew. Long Branch was hailed during his presidency as the nation's warm-weather capital, but his place was hardly a summer White House as Grant came to relax, not work.

Recounting Grant at the shore runs two perils: firstly, anecdotes retold over generations are at the risk of repetition through fading memories and exaggeration; secondly, while contemporary accounts are typically preferable, some about Grant were marred by political bias. Grant's residence at 991 Ocean Avenue adjoined George W. Childs (see page 107), his friend, benefactor and confidant. While Grant initially claimed that his funds paid for his house, after it was revealed that the place was the gift of Childs and associates, controversy ensued. His critics claimed that Grant's extensive time away from Washington was at the neglect of his duties, but Grant was a delegator and did not leave the capital until the usual congressional recess by the start of July.

When Grant visited Long Branch prior to his election, he usually stayed at the Stetson House. Acclaimed as a Civil War hero, he was thrust into the social scene. After he became a cottage owner, he was in the habit of spending time on his porch, in view of an admiring public and accessible to them. Grant preferred the ocean to the obligatory hops and balls. The resort of Long Branch was distinguished by its attractive surroundings and network of paths and trails. Grant regularly took to the roads, his carriage driven by magnificent steed. Grant the horseman kept a stock farm near St. Louis. The *New York Tribune* described his local equine facility on September 13, 1872, including the stables "behind his cottage near the public road…not large, only affording accommodations for the seven horses (then) there." The family carriage horses were handsome bays, including one notably tall and well built. There, too, was Cincinnati, Grant's mount during the war, present largely as a "pensioner for his past services."

Grant—associated with the St. James Chapel, known now as the Church of the Presidents—is known to have worshipped both there and at St. James, Broadway. However, he was more often at the church of his Methodist wife, Julia. His travel by steamer included a known stop at Cape May, while Grant regularly rode the rails. His private car carried him to the opening of the New York and Long Branch Railroad in June 1875, while he was famously on that line at the June 20, 1882 fatal derailment at Parkers Creek between

Little Silver and Oceanport. The unhurt former president directed rescue operations.

The Grants' last years at Long Branch were difficult. Grant was ruined financially through an unwise investment in the Wall Street firm of Grant and Ward. The final drama of Grant's life—death—began here. In 1884, Grant felt a pain in his throat that he attributed to a sting from something on a just-eaten peach. Medical attention, delayed to await his vacationing doctor, revealed advanced throat cancer. Grant, who had become a writer, sold war accounts to *Century* magazine. He contemplated publishing his memoirs with that firm, but his friend Mark

President Ulysses S. Grant is the quintessential Jersey Shore president, not only for long-term residency but also for mingling with the people. *Courtesy of Elizabeth Public Library.*

Twain, upon learning of their unfavorable royalty, secured better terms for Grant. Completion of his book became Grant's final battle, as the campaign was essential to provide an income for Julia. He finished writing at his Mount McGregor, New York home four days prior to his death.

Franklin Pierce (1804–1869)

Franklin Pierce may hold the distinction as the most obscure person to sit in the executive office, although adherents of his predecessor, Millard Fillmore, may take issue. Pierce does have the honor of having been the first president to vacation on the Jersey Shore.

While much of early Cape May's patronage was from Washington, the distance may have appeared great for a sitting president, as there was no capability at the time to respond quickly to control emerging crises. After three bureau chiefs in the Department of the Interior resigned, the *New York Times* grumbled on July 6, 1855, "While the country is thus losing important officers at a critical moment, it has also lost its president. President Pierce is at Cape May. For practical purposes he might as well be at Cape Horn, since he cannot by any possibility proceed to the appointment of successors for his retiring corps without the advice of his cabinet." They were right, as there was no capability to "telegraph-conference."

Pierce stayed at Congress Hall, reportedly for a ten-day visit. City officials gave a grand reception as thousands crowded streets for a glimpse. A study reported not long prior to publication of this book demonstrated that the public has little awareness of presidents other than those in their own memories, founding fathers or those in office during times of great crises. Thus, let Pierce be remembered at the shore.

Perhaps the greatest presidential impression at the shore was by a spouse as Mary Lincoln's 1861 visit to Long Branch helped propel that city to a period of preeminence on the shore. James A. Garfield's visit to Long Branch was poignant. His final trip to the shore was intended to foster healing after he was struck by an assailant's bullet, but he died in Long Branch on September 19, 1881. Recent analysis suggests that his death was likely caused by incompetent medical care.

WOODROW WILSON (1856-1924)

Wilson is the president with the greatest number of Jersey Shore associations, but he had a head start as New Jersey governor. Wilson's having conducted his 1916 reelection campaign from the Shadow Lawn porch is classic presidential lore.

Born in Staunton, Virginia, Wilson, a graduate of Princeton, had served as the university's president since 1902, when, as an untested politician, the New Jersey reform movement of 1910 swept him into the governorship. The office had a summer retreat at the National Guard base in Sea Girt, which provided a springboard for seasonal activities. In July 1911, Wilson visited Stone Harbor to dedicate a road and drawbridge. The next month, he attended President Taft's talk at the Great Auditorium in Ocean Grove. An elementary school is named for Wilson in nearby Neptune City.

Wilson's nomination for the presidency in 1912 changed the character of the Sea Girt Governor's Mansion as reporters and visitors descended. At times, Wilson sought respite at his friend Melvin A. Rice's home in the Leonardo section of Middletown on Raritan Bay. Wilson left from there in September, as he sailed from Atlantic Highlands on the yacht of his closest intimate, Cleveland Dodge, to prepare his acceptance speech while on the Atlantic. He spent a night in Wildwood at J. Thompson Baker's house, now a National Register property owned by the Wildwood Civic Club. Wilson defeated President Taft in November, aided by former president Theodore Roosevelt's Bull Moose campaign, which split the Republican vote.

In 1916, Wilson believed the war in Europe was a reason to constrain his movements, so he chose to conduct his reelection campaign from his leased summer house, Shadow Lawn. His campaign rented offices in Asbury Park. While here, Wilson helped handle that summer's Jersey Shore shark attack scare.

After Wilson dined at the Greyhound Inn on his September 8 return from Atlantic City, management treated his dining room as a shrine. While Wilson is associated with the Ocean Avenue, Long Branch St. James Chapel, known as the Church of the Presidents, he is known to have visited only the main St. James edifice on Broadway, where a commemorative plaque marks the pew he occupied on October 8, 1916. In November, Wilson secured a victory over Charles Evans Hughes in a race so close that he did not know until the following morning that he had won.

President Woodrow Wilson, front center in the dark suit, who visited the Jersey Shore as governor, is pictured at the Monmouth County Fair with officials Melvin Rice, far left, and J.A. Haskell, second from right. *Courtesy of Red Bank Public Library.*

After the original Shadow Lawn mansion was destroyed by fire in 1927, its replacement was also named Shadow Lawn. The second Shadow Lawn, now the key building on the campus of Monmouth University and named Woodrow Wilson Hall, was designated a National Historic Landmark in 1985 for the Wilson association.

PUBLIC OFFICIALS

JOSEPH AZZOLINA (1926-2010)

One crosses from the mainland to the northern tip of the Jersey Shore barrier beach by spanning the Captain Joseph Azzolina Memorial Bridge from Highlands. The naming honor reflects his lifelong service to the country, along with lifelong accomplishments in business and public benefactions.

The future captain, who began his naval career with 1949 enrollment in the Reserve Officers Training Corps, returned to active duty in the Korean War, which he followed with long service in the Naval Reserve. Joe returned to action on the battleship *New Jersey* during the 1983 Lebanon crises as a special assistant to the captain.

Joe's parents, John and Angelina, had a small grocery in Highlands, which Joe and his relatives expanded into a superette. The business evolved over the decades to the Food Circus Super Markets, part of the Foodtown chain. The Azzolina stores were regularly in the vanguard of retail innovation.

Azzolina spent three spells in the New Jersey State Assembly, to which he was first elected in 1965, first serving from 1966 to 1972, and one in the state senate, where he served in 1972 and 1973. He returned to the assembly for the 1986–87 term and then again in 1992 for a fourteen-year span during which he held major committee posts. Following retirement from elective office, Joe held significant appointed positions.

Joe was esteemed for his many benefactions and received numerous awards that reflected his charitable work along with his business and public service

Joseph Azzolina was renowned for public service, business accomplishments, a military career and his many benefactions.

accomplishments. He attained the rank of captain in the Naval Reserve in 1978. One of his most satisfying achievements was leading the campaign as chairman of the Battleship New Jersey Commission and Foundation. This resulted in the delivery of the much-decorated warship to a permanent port in its namesake state. This ship, one of the most powerful ever built, one that served from World War II through Vietnam and off Lebanon, is now a museum on the Delaware River at Camden.

Many of his gifts and contributions to children and his community are little- or unknown to the public. His enrichment of local life was the accomplishment of which Joseph Azzolina was most proud.

Alfred Nash Beadleston (1912–2000)

Alfred Nash Beadleston's family was prominent in industrial and social circles. His grandfather and father were brewers, the latter both a resident of Rumson and a principal of Beadleston and Woertz of New York, while his mother, the former Helen Hazard, was a daughter of the famed Shrewsbury ketchup and condiments manufacturer Edward C. Hazard. Their son would make his mark in public service.

Beadleston was immersed in his career overseeing the family's real estate firm, which the prohibition-shut brewery holdings had evolved into, when unexpectedly in 1938 he was asked to fill a need and run for the Shrewsbury borough council. Following his election, he served in that post and later as mayor prior to election to the New Jersey State Assembly in 1951 and state senate in 1967. He served sixteen and ten years respectively, attaining selection as assembly speaker and senate president. During World War II, he was area director of New Jersey Civil Defense.

Beadleston, a full-time legislator, attained respect for his knowledge of every bill and ability to work successfully within a partisan system. His legislative record included action on water supply, highway construction and safety, prison reform and the laws of municipalities. His signature bill, which became known as the Beadleston Law, mandated state-provided education for handicapped children. This accomplishment alone would have brought him enduring stature. All other states followed the New Jersey lead. After Beadleston retired at the end of 1977, he kept his vow to stay out of politics.

Alfred N. Beadleston, the consummate legislator, built a world-class seashell collection, which has entered a museum.

He and wife Isabel became extensive world travelers, while the senator became a collector and student of the globe's seashells. Beadleston's massive collection of about thirty-four thousand catalogued specimens was donated to the Bailey-Matthews Shell Museum, Sanibel, Florida, where it serves his lifelong dedication to education.

OLIVER HUFF BROWN (1852–1924)

Brown is represented by a building, his munificent gift to his town made near the end of his life, a gesture that has enriched Spring Lake cultural life for nearly a century.

Born in Farmingdale, Brown began his career as a retail employee prior to opening his own furniture store, the first of many business ventures, notably in the hotel and banking fields. A former resident of Asbury Park, he was an organizer of a number of financial institutions there and its Monterrey Hotel. He was also active in Lakewood and Bradley Beach, but his principal focus was Spring Lake.

Oliver H. Brown, after long and successful careers in business and elective office, is memorialized in Spring Lake by his gift of a community center and library.

Brown's local hotel interests included both the New Monmouth and the Essex and Sussex. He was an organizer and later president of the First National Bank of Spring Lake.

Politically, after the organization of the borough, Brown served on the first council and then was mayor, a post he held for about twenty years. After election to the New Jersey Assembly in 1897, he served one term there prior to four terms in the state senate.

Oliver Brown planned his gift as early as 1919. He acquired the northwest corner of Third and Madison Avenues to build the community center that combines a theatre and library. The cornerstone of the Tudor Revival building, designed by Frank E. Newman of New York and erected as a memorial to our war veterans, was laid in March 1922 prior to its dedication on July 4, 1923. While Brown died less than a year later, his magnificent building and gesture is a gift that keeps giving.

JANE G. CLAYTON (B. 1928)

Jane Clayton's long public service left a legacy of New Jersey's finest county record storage system and activism in history, achievements that the County of Monmouth recognizes by the annual bestowal of the Jane G. Clayton Award. She also achieved notable electoral firsts.

Clayton may have inherited political genes, as her father, Eugene Gardella, served as a Sea Bright councilman, while her mother, Dorothy, was a county committeewoman from the same town. She claimed an early start in political life by serving while a youth at teas hosted by the legendary Republican stalwart Geraldine Thompson.

Clayton's office holding began in 1966 on the Monmouth County Board of Elections, while her elective career began in 1976 when she was chosen as the first woman voted to the Monmouth County Board of Chosen Freeholders. She defeated short-term incumbent Cecile Norton, who had been appointed earlier that year to fill a vacancy. Her trendsetting was replicated three years later when she was elected as Monmouth's first female county clerk, an office to which she was reelected in 1984, 1989 and 1994. Clayton's signature accomplishment was achieved in this office.

A county clerk's responsibilities include maintenance of public records, which, in addition to the myriad contemporary transactions, embraces historical documents. Having perceived that storage of the latter was haphazard at best,

Jane G. Clayton, a pioneer in Monmouth County elective office, built a model records storage facility that two decades later is still the most effective of its type.

Clayton sought to elevate their preservation in a state-of-the-art facility, which was accomplished via a freeholder-approved proposal to build a records storage system as part of a new county library building in Manalapan. Document relocation there began in 1987 in the facility that is esteemed as a model of its type. One rare document, inauspiciously labeled "Slave Book," after its careful analysis and organization, resulted in two major publications by her office, the *Black Birth Book of Monmouth County* and the *Manumission Book of Monmouth County* in 1989 and 1992 respectively. The archives continue to expand accessibility to records and engage in the preservation of a wider variety of historical materials. Its holdings have aided legions of historians and genealogists.

While Clayton maintained an officership in the family business, Eugene and Company, a wholesale institutional grocery provisioner, she was a full-time county clerk until her retirement at the end of 1996. Her advocacy for history and accomplishments in preservation are recognized each year with the designation of the Jane G. Clayton Award to an individual with a record of achievement in Monmouth County history.

JAMES MELVILLE COLEMAN JR. (1924–2014)

Coleman, known even in his mature years as Chippy, first attained fame as an Asbury Park High School athlete where he was twice an all-state basketball player and holder of the outdoor half-mile record in track. After World War II Army Air Corps service in Italy and the earning of a law degree, he began a long, distinguished career in public service.

Coleman was a practicing lawyer when first elected to office in 1957, the Asbury Park City Council, on which he served until 1965, the year prior to his election to the New Jersey State Assembly. Following reelection twice, Coleman was appointed Monmouth County prosecutor for the years 1972–1977. He took pride and satisfaction in the office, having brought to trial 123 out of the 125 homicides in the county during that period and for the later successes of the assistant prosecutors who served under him. From 1977 to 1980, he served in the office of the New Jersey Legislative Reviser of Statutes, which he called the best job he ever had. Coleman was appointed judge in the Superior Court, Monmouth County Juvenile and Domestic Relations, a position held until retirement in 1987. There followed from 1998 to 2007 service on the Joint Legislative Committee on Ethical Standards. Coleman's final appointment was to the library board at Middletown Township, where I had the privilege of serving with this voice of dignity, experience and wisdom.

Coleman was honored by his alma mater, Dartmouth College, which he served in various capacities. He was predeceased by his first wife, the former Dolores Kassak. Chippy is enshrined in two shore athletic halls of fame and in the Asbury Park High School Hall of Fame, as is his second wife, Judith Stanley Coleman.

JUDITH STANLEY COLEMAN (c. 1935–2010)

Asbury Park native Judy Stanley Coleman, née Hurley, after studying history at Smith, became a historic model for public service. She was one of the foremost conservationists of her era.

After a brief spell as a teacher in Asbury Park, where her grandfather Harrison C. Hurley was a twenty-five-year president of the board of education, Judith, valedictorian of the class of 1952, married Anthony Huber and left to raise their four daughters. She undertook her political and charitable activism in the early 1970s while married to Robert C. Stanley Jr., a key figure in the nickel metals industry. By then a resident of Middletown, her longest and most crucial public position was on the township's planning board. She served as chair for most of her nearly thirty years as an ardent advocate of policies for sound growth and preservation of open space.

Coleman was a founder and long-term president of the Monmouth Conservation Foundation, which serves as an intermediate and funder in the acquisition of open space. This was one of her most cherished positions for the ability to quantify responsibility for land preservation. In 1992, she received their Verdant Award for her major preservation contributions.

Coleman's most visible appointment was her five-year chairmanship of the New Jersey Highway Authority, a spell during the 1980s when they improved the roads and service areas of the Garden State Parkway and

Judith Stanley Coleman fulfilled her Asbury Park classmates' designation of "most likely to succeed" with an outstanding career in public service, charitable work and conservation.

earned a profit for their arts center. Much of her service work was devoted to health and education. Coleman was closely identified with the Visiting Nurse Association of Central Jersey (formerly MCOSS), having served on its board for nearly fifty years, most as president. She was the first recipient of their Robert Crooks Stanley Jr. Humanitarian Award, named for her second husband, who died in 1985. The VNA headquarters building in Red Bank is named for her. She was also a longtime trustee of Monmouth Medical Center and the Monmouth Medical Center Foundation.

In the educational-cultural world, Coleman served on the boards of the Monmouth County Historical Association, including long tenure as president, the New Jersey State Council on the Arts, Monmouth University, Stevens Institute of Technology (which awarded her an honorary engineering degree), the Count Basie Theatre and Rumson Country Day School.

One of Coleman's main aspirations was to leave the world a better place for future generations, a goal she accomplished as an effective force for land preservation. This profile of a lengthy but partial enumeration of organizational affiliations reflects her chosen life of service. Also a gracious hostess, Coleman amply fulfilled her class selection as "most likely to succeed." She along with husband James M. Coleman entered the Asbury Park High School Hall of Fame in 2004.

FRANK S. FARLEY (1901-1977)

Frank Farley had a tough act to follow—Nucky Johnson (see page 100)—which required him to demonstrate considerable political acumen to attain the position of Atlantic County Republican leader. The office would be under close scrutiny, both by regulators and potential rivals. Farley not only successfully consolidated power, he also managed to remain in the New Jersey State Legislature for a record thirty-four years, three in the state assembly and the remainder in the state senate. The profound changes that evolved during his times ushered Farley's eventual fall.

Born in Atlantic City, Farley, a three-sport athlete in high school, started for the Georgetown basketball team while in law school. He maintained his athletic interests after his admission to the bar as he honed his skills for teamwork and sealed friendships that would serve him well in politics. The Atlantic County party leadership would be earned rather than inherited and would go to one who would learn to master the needs and workings of both politicians and racketeers. Although then a member of the state senate, Hap, as he was known, rose by securing the aid of potential rivals.

Farley's command of the political process came through deft deal making and steadfast reliability for keeping his word. Two key accomplishments were securing approval for parimutuel betting at racetracks and approval of bond issues for toll roads and county colleges. Changing times hurt Farley, especially the 1964 *Reynolds v. Sims* New Jersey Supreme Court decision that mandated proportional representation in the state senate to replace the existing senate make-up of one senator from each county; the power of southern New Jersey was thus diluted. The decline of the Atlantic City resort cost Farley. As the city, long ago frayed at the edges, deteriorated at the core, old alliances weakened. Farley initially opposed casino gambling, which had been proposed as a cure to the city's ills, a position that further distanced him from a changing electorate. Farley, who was defeated in his 1971 reelection bid by a Democrat who was able to garner Republican support, would have benefited from foresight that would have told him that times were changing while he was not.

JOEL HAYWOOD (1798–1865)

Born in West Creek, Eagleswood Township, the self-educated Haywood both followed his father's calling as a blacksmith and became ordained a minister prior to his attainment of prominence in public life.

Haywood, cited as the most active spokesperson for the formation of a new county, is esteemed as the founder of the County of Ocean, an entity separated from the County of Monmouth in 1850 by a vote in the state legislature made along party lines. When it was suggested two years later that part of Ocean's territory be returned to Monmouth, Haywood forcefully opposed any concession.

Haywood, who first served in the New Jersey State Assembly in 1842 and had been a justice of the peace, was Ocean's first member of that body in 1851. He later was the Whig candidate for governor in 1853. After he lost, his candidacy marred by his pro-temperance stance, he protested the winner's eligibility to serve based on a residency issue, one that did not deny the victor the statehouse. Haywood, who was active in the organization of the Republican Party in 1854, was later considered as a congressional

Joel Haywood is esteemed as "the father of Ocean County." This courthouse was built shortly after the county's 1850 formation.

candidate but was not nominated. He appeared to spend the next decade as a private citizen prior to a term on the Ocean County Board of Chosen Freeholders from 1862.

JAMES J. HOWARD (1927-1985)

The election of Jim Howard to the House of Representatives was not expected. However, after he arrived, propelled by the Lyndon B. Johnson landslide victory in 1964, he remained a fixture there for the rest of his life.

Born in Irvington, New Jersey, Howard was raised in Belmar and received his primary education at St. Rose and secondary education at nearby Asbury Park High School. This navy veteran of World War II became a teacher, union activist and acting principal in the Wall Township system. The Third Congressional District, known at the time as the "shore district," had long been regarded as solidly Republican. James C. Auchincloss, its long-serving stalwart, planned to retire prior to the start of the January term. Howard was the surprise winner.

Howard became a master of the political process, earning esteem as one who knew how to get results in a partisan arena. As he rose to the chairmanship of

James J. Howard was a surprise winner in his first congressional election, but once in office, he remained for life.

the Committee on Public Works and Transportation, Howard became a tireless advocate for transportation; he was also principal backer of the former national fifty-five-miles-per-hour speed limit. He is honored for his accomplishments in the field by the naming of Interstate 195, which runs across central New Jersey, as the James J. Howard Interstate Highway. The Asbury Park train and bus station is also named for him.

Howard was an ardent foe of ocean dumping. Following the 1985 destruction by fire of the Northeast Fisheries Science Center at Sandy Hook, a rebuilt research laboratory was named the James J. Howard Marine Sciences Laboratory.

Howard faced numerous electoral challenges in his long career, always winning, albeit at times narrowly. After his premature death caused by a heart ailment, he was replaced by Frank Pallone in a now reconstituted district.

Enoch (Nucky) L. Johnson (1883-1968)

Nucky Johnson's spirit may rue his recent rise in recognition. While the popular fictionalized television series *Boardwalk Empire* made his name virtually a household word, the life and times of the real Nucky were more efficient and less violent than their fictional counterparts.

Johnson's first office, Atlantic County Undersheriff under his father Smith Johnson in 1905, was followed by sheriff in 1908. Subsequently, in 1913, he attained the office that he would hold for decades, which he used as his seat of power, Atlantic County treasurer. Johnson seized leadership after the reigning boss, Louis Kuehnle, was jailed for corruption. Johnson's public profile was elevated following his 1916 role in the election of Walter Edge as governor. Edge named Johnson clerk of the state supreme court. Once in the role, Johnson became the consummate urban political boss.

While popular promotion called Atlantic City "America's Favorite Playground," the place's real draw was less beach and boardwalk and more gambling, liquor and sex. Operations that flouted the law created ample opportunities for graft and payoffs. The ruling organization was awash with protection money. Illicit activity, prevalent in the early decades of the twentieth century, reached new heights—depths may be a better term—with the 1921 onset of prohibition. Access to alcohol may have been a sub-rosa practice in most places, but the booze flowed openly and freely in Atlantic City, all to the prosperity of the organization.

Johnson was a tough, effective administrator who realized that power was maintained through addressing the needs of his people and minions. His outsized life and career cannot be briefly summarized. The best account of his times is Nelson Johnson's 2002 book *Boardwalk Empire*, a scholarly, insightful tome belied by the show that bought the title and dropped the scholarship. Authorities tried long and hard to take down Nucky; they finally succeeded with a 1941 conviction for tax evasion. Following Johnson's four years in prison, he lived an uneventful life with his second wife, whom he married ten days prior to being jailed. He was employed in sales and never again sought office, although he would appear at political events; he died in a convalescent home.

JAMES J. MANCINI SR. (1926–2003)

Mancini was the consummate populist politician. During his nearly four decades in public office, Long Beach Island and the treatment of the environment were transformed. However, it is apparent that this builder turned elected official found the changes difficult to embrace.

The Newark native's first glimpse of the island in 1950 convinced him that this then little-known and less-pricy shore spot was an alternative that spelled opportunity. This realization was reinforced when he learned one could build there in winter, as the ground was not frozen. After Mancini decided to stay full time, he became a leading developer on the island. The 1950s and 1960s were a time when the old real estate saw "they are not making any more land" was regularly flouted by extensive fill operations. This environmentally harmful practice was ended by the Wetlands Act of 1970, but by then, Mancini owned

James Mancini, a populist politician-developer from Long Beach, experienced profound change in office, notably after he learned that Barnegat Bay would not be filled in forever. *Courtesy of Margaret Buchholz.*

no more wetlands. However, he cited with sympathetic understanding the legality of owners filling in until the last legal moment. He reflected in 1994 that "in those days it was the proper—it was the right thing to do." His complaint was the need to take the blame for the resultant problems as mayor of Long Beach Township.

Mancini was elected a township commissioner in 1964 and then mayor the next year, an office he held until his death. The unrestrained operative was known as "the kissing mayor" and for his penchant for uninhibited talk. He was also elected to the Ocean County Board of Chosen Freeholders in 1982, a position he held for the rest of his life, and served one term in the state assembly. He received many honors and held numerous public, business and organizational positions. He seemed to prefer the earlier times as when he was building inspector and could remind people moving into a new house to come in for a permit. Mancini believed the shoreline was to be fixed in its developed state, calling those who would remedy building lines "pseudo-environmentalists." However, even as the times and conditions evolved, an unchanged Mancini remained himself to a public that returned him to office for nearly forty years.

THOMAS A. MATHIS (1869–1958)

Mathis, a New Gretna, Burlington County native and son of a sea captain, began his maritime career in 1885 and rose to secure licensure to navigate any type vessel. Acclimating to the rough, rigorous conditions at sea no doubt served him well in his second career, the maelstrom of Ocean County politics.

Mathis claimed to have plied the waters until 1915, but he was active in Tuckerton politics by the early twentieth century, reportedly having been elected to the newly incorporated borough's first council. He served three years from 1906 as a member of the New Jersey Board of Pilot Commissioners. Mathis, who had earlier secured an automobile dealership in Philadelphia, relocated around 1908 to Toms River, where he became a Ford dealer. His insurance agency opened in Tuckerton, a business that would become lucrative, especially after Mathis could cultivate political business.

Captain Tom, as he was widely known, had a difficult beginning in state office. He was first elected to the state senate in 1909 to fill a vacancy that resulted from the death of William J. Harrison. However, after he appeared to have won the 1910 campaign, an election marred by accusations of ballot stuffing, resultant litigation forced him out of his seat. Three years later, after a recount, he won by the thinnest of margins, but he apparently retained the

seat for only one term. Mathis, who was back in the senate in the 1920s, was elected president of that body in 1929, the first from Ocean County to receive that honor. Governor Moore appointed him to officerships in the New Jersey Naval Militia. Mathis was also appointed New Jersey secretary of state in 1931 and reappointed in 1936. After reformist Democrat Charles Edison did not retain him, Mathis was chosen Ocean County treasurer in 1942 prior to a return to the senate. He also owned the newspaper *Ocean County Sun*, which became a lucrative source of government advertising.

Thomas Mathis, after transitioning from a maritime career to Ocean County politics, ruled his county for decades as king. *Courtesy of Ocean County Historical Society.*

Mathis, as astute a politician as there was, embraced inclusiveness of all county Republican allies.

However, he could leave Ocean Democrats unmentioned, while he made mutually beneficial deals with their northern New Jersey counterparts. Esteemed by the locals, they named their organizations Thomas A. Mathis or TAM Republican Clubs, a following that assured control and power tantamount to a king. The support of these tightknit organizations did not waver despite numerous charges of wrongdoing against Mathis. Loyalty was mutual and intense.

The post–World War II period changed suburban New Jersey, albeit the process and growth were relatively slow in rural Ocean County. Rooted in the ways of the past, Mathis either did not or could not change with the times. While he once envisioned living to one hundred, he took his life with a self-inflicted gunshot eleven years short of that goal. The eastbound Highway 37 bridge over Barnegat Bay is named in his honor.

RESIDENTS AND VISITORS

NATHANIEL HOLMES BISHOP (1837-1902)

Bishop, a Medford, Massachusetts native, became renowned for his hemisphere-wide adventures but settled in Manahawkin to be near Barnegat Bay and the Jersey Shore.

By age seventeen, Bishop set out on a one-thousand-mile hike across lower South America, which in 1869 was depicted in his first book, *The Pampas and Andes: A Thousand Mile Walk Across South America.* Apparently having previously resided in Lacey Township, after the aforementioned relocation, he raised cranberries, a crop that by Bishop's time had become locally lucrative (see page 27). While there, he discovered the canoe, a recreational craft newly introduced from England. Bishop ordered a substantial wood model that, fully outfitted, weighed in at three hundred pounds. Naming it the *Mayetta* for a section of Stafford, he set out with intentions to journey from Quebec to the mouth of the Gulf of Mexico in Florida. However, the heavy boat was too unwieldy. Bishop then bought a newly developed, easily repairable, pressure-laminated paper variety in which he left Manahawkin in 1874 for Florida, rowing along sections of what would emerge as the Intracoastal Waterway. That trip was chronicled in *Voyage of the Paper Canoe.*

Subsequently, Bishop discovered a small boat developed for Barnegat Bay gunning use. The evolving craft, called a sneakbox, had recently found a popular following, although Hazleton Seaman's prototype, which he built for his own use, dated back to about 1836. After Bishop sailed his specially built twelve- by four-foot sneakbox to Florida via the Ohio and Mississippi Rivers, he wrote about his adventure in *Four Months in a Sneakbox*.

Bishop settled on Water Street, Toms River. Most of his estate was left for the establishment of a public library for which Toms River (then Dover Township) honored him by naming it the Bishop Memorial Library. Reporters have regularly recounted Bishop's story. Other than in his own works, a researched account appears to have first been written in Peter J. Guthorn's 1971 *The Sea Bright Skiff and Other Jersey Shore Boats*.

JOHN V.A. CATTUS (1867–1945)

The name John V.A. Cattus would ordinarily delight a researcher, as it may be unique. After a diligent search, one wonders how the patronym of a county park so prominent can remain historically obscure.

John's father, also John, was a German immigrant who arrived in 1859 and prospered as a tobacco broker in New York, where the family also lived. The son, an importer of Asian goods, has been described as dealing in Siberian dog hair and Canton china. In addition, contemporary accounts took note that he paid particular attention to brush materials; he also handled Japanese baskets. His mention in the trade journals *Hides and Shoes* and *Woolen and Woolen Ware Trade Review*, makes one suspect he also dealt in those goods.

Cattus, resident at 508 West End Avenue, New York, bought the approximately four-hundred-acre island in 1895. His intended recreational use included hunting and fishing. One presumes he was prosperous, but by 1907, Cattus was bankrupt; his major creditors included Emma Embury Cattus, reportedly an aunt. He retained stature in the trade as he served for some years thereafter as an arbitrator.

Cattus raced boats, especially the sneakbox type that was developed for local waters. He was the first commodore of the Bay Head Yacht Club. Cattus shared his passion with his daughter Louise, known as Lulu, who won in 1911 a local women's one-design boat race in her father's craft. Perhaps married twice, Cattus survived the former Louise Baber, who died in 1936; their children were John C., Charles B. and Louise B. Wells.

First Lieutenant John C. Cattus was awarded the Distinguished Service Cross for extraordinary heroism during the First World War. After a severe wound, he returned to his command post to assist with information on enemy troop movements. An athlete and member of the

New York Athletic Club, he was a member of the 1928 United States Olympic water polo team.

Cattus is buried in Pottsville, Pennsylvania, at the Charles Baber Cemetery. The family retained his waterfront lodge for years but sold it to the County of Ocean in 1964. As late as 1963, Louise Cattus raced for the Bay Head Yacht Club. Over time, perhaps additional research will flesh out the biography of John V.A. Cattus so the life will be as familiar as the recreation area.

GEORGE W. CHILDS (1829-1894)

One could call Childs "the man who knew presidents," as he was friends with several and, at the Jersey Shore, particularly close to Grant. Although during his lifetime Childs was esteemed as Philadelphia publisher of the *Public Ledger*, the memory of this Gilded Age stalwart has since faded, but his accomplishments merit burnishing his historical record.

Childs was born in Baltimore, the illegitimate child of a prominent father, but little is known of his early years as Childs guarded his past. He joined the navy while a youth, worked in a bookstore afterward and, while still in his teens, opened a retail business. After Childs took employment with publishing firms, he rose to partner, earning respect through diligent, honest work. During this time, he admired the *Public Ledger* and even aspired to own it.

The *Ledger* became a money loser after the start of the Civil War, its profitability constrained by war-prompted rising costs and a decline in public following that stemmed from the paper's failure to back the Union. Childs, with his longtime financier and intimate Anthony J. Drexel, purchased the paper at a distressed price and then changed editorial policy to pro-Union. Childs, through direct, personal involvement, not only made the publication profitable, but also turned the paper into one of the nation's most respected.

Their differences in background and personality appear to make the link between publisher and military hero–future president unlikely. Regardless of how their tie occurred, perhaps through Grant's contemplation of his postwar memoirs, his presidential power and Childs's wealth mixed well for their mutual betterment, especially for Grant's ownership of his homes. Contemporary accounts suggest Grant made a personal purchase of his substantial Ocean Avenue, Long Branch summer house, but a Childs-led business team was behind the funding. They replicated this practice for Grant elsewhere. How

George W. Childs, a successful publisher, was not only "the man who knew presidents," but also had daily contact with next door neighbor Ulysses S. Grant. *Courtesy of Karen L. Schnitzspahn.*

close were the two? Grant was next door with nary a fence separating their joint spreads; contact was daily.

Childs knew all the presidents from Andrew Johnson through Grover Cleveland. While he did not aspire for office, Childs was seriously considered for a presidential nomination in 1888. He was honored for his many benefactions. Childs and Drexel were engaged in public improvement, having bought land for the early planned community of Wayne, Pennsylvania. Childs succeeded Drexel as the second president of the latter's namesake university. He donated land for a state park in the Pocono area of Pennsylvania, which is now the George W. Childs Recreation Site, located in the Delaware Water Gap National Recreation Area. He funded a number of monuments and donated land in Philadelphia for a cemetery for printers. A beloved giant in his time, the Pennsylvania "man who knew presidents" also made his mark on the Jersey Shore.

Dr. Ernest Fahnestock (1876–1937)

Fahnestock (his family pronounced it Fan-stock), a noted surgeon at what is now Monmouth Medical Center, Long Branch, built one of the region's finest country estates. While the Fahnestock Shrewsbury residence has become famed as a restaurant-catering venue, his distinguished life merits commemoration.

Ernest, born in New York the son of the influential banker Harris, graduated from Columbia as a physician in 1900 in the same class with his brother Clarence. He resided in New York and held posts with a number of hospitals there. Fahnestock became familiar with Monmouth County from his family's Long Branch oceanfront cottage well prior to his purchase of Shrewsbury farm property in 1908. He built a farm group on it, following the fashion of the time. A fine Colonial Revival residence was its centerpiece, a home accompanied by a dairy, a U-shaped carriage house-stable, a superintendent's house and the typical outbuildings. He named the estate Shadow Brook for the shadows cast by tall trees through a property bisected by a stream. Fahnestock's estate, designed by noted county house specialists Albro and Lindeberg, helped stabilize a community where small houses were encroaching from Red Bank to the north.

Fahnestock, a leading surgeon at Monmouth Medical, was also a major patron and member of its governing body, which he served ten years as president. He was a benefactor of many local organizations, including Shrewsbury's fire company and Christ Church. His beneficence also aided many New York recipients. Following Clarence's death in 1918 from pneumonia while serving with the army in France during World War I, Ernest gave the former's estate, also designed by Albro and Lindeberg, and two thousand acres to the State of New York for use as a park.

Ernest and his wife, the former Georgette De Grove Perry, had two daughters. He ended his life with a self-inflicted gunshot. His widow, who retained Shadow Brook for several years as the Great Depression

Dr. Ernest Fahnestock, a successful surgeon, built Shadowbrook in Shrewsbury, one of the region's finest country estates. *Courtesy of Shrewsbury Historical Society.*

killed the market for large estates, sold it for a virtual pittance in 1942. After Fred Thorngreen opened a restaurant in the house in 1943, its name was given the single word spelling of Shadowbrook, apparently by inadvertence in a newspaper advertisement. Gerard Keller was an interim owner prior to the Zweben family's purchase in 1971. They raised the elegance of the establishment and then later began to specialize in weddings and catered events.

MARTIN MALONEY (1847-1929)

Martin Maloney, who emigrated from Ireland as a young boy, rose from youthful work in coal mines to become a powerful, wealthy Philadelphia industrialist. A Spring Lake summer resident, his expression of grief at one of the lowest moments of his life gave the Jersey Shore its finest twentieth-century house of worship.

As a young man, Maloney opened a grocery store in Scranton, Pennsylvania, near the mines he had worked. An investor in gas, plumbing and heating, his inventiveness developed a gasoline burner for use in streetlights. Staying in the forefront of the changing gas and lighting businesses, Maloney's fortune was enhanced by profits from his Standard Oil investment. After Maloney foresaw the future of electricity for lighting, he directed his investments to this emerging power source. He used his wealth for many benefactions, notably for Catholic causes here and abroad.

Maloney helped restore the home church of the Bishop of Rome, St. John Lateran. He funded anonymously the retention of French convents after the government closed them. Pope Leo XIII designated Maloney a papal marquis, while Pope Pius X appointed him a chamberlain at the papal court. Other gifts funded a home for the aged in Scranton; a chemical laboratory at Catholic University, District of Columbia; and a clinic at the University of Pennsylvania.

Maloney married the former Margaret Hewittson in 1868. Decades later, they built their summer home, a White House lookalike that he named Ballingarry for his home county in Ireland. Of their three daughters, Margaret, Helen and Catharine, the latter did not enjoy a robust constitution. She traveled with her mother and elder sister Margaret in an unsuccessful attempt to restore her health, but at seventeen, she died at sea on May 20, 1900.

Martin Maloney's memorial to his daughter in Spring Lake is the Jersey Shore's finest twentieth-century house of worship, St. Catharine Church.

The Maloneys donated a church as her memorial, using architect Horace Trumbauer who had designed their residence. The local parish, previously St. Ann's Catholic Church (as the name was spelled then) was renamed Catharine in her honor. The richly decorated Beaux-Arts/Classical Revival edifice stands as both architectural and artistic treasure.

NORMAN L. MUNRO (1842–1894)

Nova Scotia native Munro, who amassed a fortune through popular publishing ventures, notably dime novels and *Munro's Magazine*, once one of the nation's leading periodicals, had a passion for fast motor yachts, notably his *Norwood*. The vessel's name was replicated in his exclusive Jersey Shore development, Norwood Park.

Munro's first land purchase, about 9 acres that included the cottage of the famed actress Mary Anderson at the northwest corner of Cedar and Norwood

Avenues, was expanded through subsequent purchases to about 250 acres. Munro fashioned his development after John Hoey's (see page 126) Hollywood. Munro moved Anderson's place to a nearby location and built on its site his fine residence, which he called Normahurst after his daughter, Norma L. The colony sported a 150-foot observation tower, the tallest structure in the county at the time; finely landscaped grounds; athletic fields, including a saddle track; and a casino, which was the center of social life. Twenty cottages were built for Norwood Park's 1889 opening.

Munro's unexpected death following an operation for appendicitis cost him the opportunity to complete his grand plan. He was survived by his widow, Henrietta; Norma; and son Henry. Normahurst, which became a rental, holds a minor footnote in presidential lore. The place was leased to one political notable, Vice President

Norman Munro, a successful publisher, planned a high-class country development that he did not live to see come to fruition.

Garret A. Hobart, who was photographed there in 1899 with President William McKinley during what is believed to have been the only confirmed visit of the latter to Long Branch during his presidency.

After Normahurst was destroyed by fire in 1902, its lot was bought by Murry Guggenheim, who built the Beaux-Arts mansion that is now the core of the Monmouth University Library. Henrietta purchased a farm in Middletown located near the author's home but lost it a few years later in a sheriff's sale. Norwood Park remains a section in the present West Long Branch, spanning north and west from the aforementioned intersection. Much of the expanse was filled in with post–World War II construction. The houses from the Munro period are readily recognizable by their size and styles, typically Queen Anne.

HUBERT TEMPLETON PARSON (1872-1940)

The historical Parson can claim stature as the builder of what is arguably the Jersey Shore's greatest mansion ever. The man Parson suffered social rejection, forced retirement and the loss of his symbol of excess.

The Toronto native, who moved to Brooklyn as a young boy and joined a fledgling Woolworth firm as a bookkeeper in 1892, became a trusted advisor to founder Frank Winfield Woolworth through his financial acumen, planning ability and command of nearly every aspect of the business. His forceful personality also aided Parson's rise through the ranks. It is said he represented the son that Woolworth never had. Parson ran the firm as a vice-president after Woolworth became disabled in 1916 and then assumed the presidency upon the latter's death in 1919.

Parson married the former Maysie Gasque, a seamstress, also from Brooklyn and the sister of a co-worker. His rise enabled them to enjoy the good life, which included apartments at 1071 Fifth Avenue, New York and on the posh Avenue Foch in Paris. Aspirations for a grand residence were fulfilled after their 1918 purchase of the Shadow Lawn I country house built by John McCall in 1902 at the southwest corner of Cedar and Norwood Avenues. The place had attained recent notoriety as the site of President Wilson's (see page 87) home-based, successful 1916 reelection campaign. However, prior owners had been struck by a series of misfortunes that one could mistake for a curse that enveloped the place. McCall lost Shadow Lawn when ensnared in a life insurance financial scandal. Bond manipulator Abraham "Postage Stamp" White was foreclosed after about two years. The 1909 purchase by New York retailer Joseph B. Greenhut gave him the longest run, but he suffered substantial business reverses prior to his 1918 death. Finally, Shadow Lawn was destroyed by fire on January 7, 1927. Parson's reconstruction not only redefined "extravagant" but also may have been an unspoken competition with his deceased master.

After Woolworth lost his Glen Cove, Long Island country place to fire, he hired a master of mansion architecture, C.P.H. Gilbert, for his 1916

Hubert Parson built Shadow Lawn II to attain social prominence, but recognition eluded him. His former residence, now part of Monmouth University, features a center hall that is little changed from Parson's time.

Beaux-Arts "Winfield Hall." While seeking a country house specialist, Parson admired Edward T. Stotesbury's Whitemarsh Hall in Pennsylvania, so he hired its architect, Horace Trumbauer, with the expectation that the resultant mansion, Shadow Lawn II, would attain for Maysie and him the elevated social status that they craved. Following numerous change orders to satisfy her every whim, the place was completed in 1930. However, much to their dismay, the Parsons were shunned at their housewarming party. After Parson reached age sixty, he found Woolworth's mandatory retirement policy was enforced for him. The loss of his salary precluded his ability to maintain Shadow Lawn. They managed to stay until 1938, but lost the place, which the Borough of West Long Branch acquired for unpaid taxes. They held on to their lavish furnishings until a spectacular 1940 auction. Two weeks later, Parson died. In time, Shadow Lawn II was acquired by Monmouth College, now University. It was adapted for educational purposes, which maintained its integrity. The building, named Woodrow Wilson Hall, attained National Historic Landmark stature in 1985 and remains as one of the Jersey Shore's greatest historic sites.

DR. EMLEN PHYSICK JR. (1855-1916)

Physick is well known in Cape May history but primarily for the Physick Estate, which is the grandest house in the city, a Stick-style structure built in 1879 at the peak of the Victorian era. However, the person is little known.

Physick trained as a physician to fulfill family expectations; his grandfather Philip Syng Physick was a prominent, even legendary, surgeon. However, Emlen hardly practiced medicine and certainly not in his later decades. Wealth that precluded the necessity of work appeared to leave Physick content to live as a gentleman. He invested in property, both in his native Philadelphia and in his family's adopted Cape May County, where he recorded many transactions and farmed one or more of his agricultural holdings. The construction of the house appears to have been a venture undertaken with his mother. The architect is unknown, but the place is so closely identified with the Philadelphia master Frank Furness that an additional repetition of an unconfirmed attribution will likely do no harm. Another Physick holding, an extensive tract near the Cold Spring Mill tract, was designated for local improvement, a subject that interested Physick. He sold nearly four hundred acres to Henry Ford for an automobile factory that never materialized. Physick also donated property for a failed clothing factory.

Physick, a clubman and sportsman, continued to maintain memberships in Philadelphia, the city he visited regularly to attend to business. They included the prestigious Union League Club. Near home, he promoted a local casino, donated land for a yacht club and was a major backer of the Cape May golf club. Physick was a gunner who owned many dogs, but he was also president of the Cape May Society for the Prevention of Cruelty to Animals.

Physick may not have possessed commercial acumen despite his backing of local businesses. Thus, it was likely a surprise when in 1904 he assumed the presidency of the failing First National Bank of Cape May. However, the position could be justified by his having had the funds to inject substantial capital. Later, when Phyick closed the bank without consulting the directors after he determined it was beyond saving, his unilateral move engendered ill will.

The unmarried Physick left no descendents. His house at 1048 Washington Street became vital to the preservation movement in Cape May. When threatened with destruction, local preservationists galvanized for its rescue. The group emerged as the Mid-Atlantic Center for the

In Cape May, "Physick" is invariably followed by "estate," understandable, as his house, now open to the public, is the finest in the city. *Courtesy of Robert Pellegrini.*

Arts, an organization that became and remains the major promoter of history and culture in Cape May County. The house is one of the county's greatest tourist highlights.

CAPTAIN EDWARD HARTSHORNE PRICE (1827–1907)

Price, a pioneer at Pleasure Bay, a North Long Branch neighborhood located on Branchport Creek, settled there when the overgrown area was visited by none but woodsmen. Price, a mariner of note, established a water sport tradition on Pleasure Bay and built there one of the Branch's legendary hostelries.

The son of John, a sailing ship captain, Edward, who went to sea as a young lad, himself became the master of vessels, both sail and steam, ships that plied the waters from Oceanport to New York. After he retired to Pleasure Bay in 1854, six years after he married the former Ann West, they erected a two-room building in 1862. Thus began their attempt to secure a business in the rough pines. "Harts," as he was called, the name preceded by an honorific "uncle" late in life, claimed to have originated "shore dinners," which were gastronomic excesses that piled on a variety of game, meats and seafood. Harts credited his wife's culinary skills for their major success, which was also aided by word of mouth from the satisfied, including praise from a sated President Grant. By late century, the place had expanded to thirty rooms.

Harts enjoyed pleasure yachting, both sail- and iceboats. A founder of the South Shrewsbury Ice Boat

Captain Edward Hartshorne Price was legendary as a restaurateur and yachtsman.

and Yacht Club (now the Long Branch Ice Boat and Yacht Club), he instructed his sons shortly before his death to donate the Price Cup as a competition award. His sons continued the business, which was a restaurant only in its later years (and located adjacent to the Pleasure Bay Bridge), until the place was closed following a fire on November 8, 1953.

MOSES TAYLOR (1806-1882)

Moses Taylor, a summer resident of Long Branch, may or may not have known he was one of the wealthiest men in America, as he did not share a balance sheet with his family. His wife, Catherine, was astonished to learn in 1882 that she had become the richest widow in the country. She honored her late husband by building a memorial that is one of the Jersey Shore's finest ecclesiastical edifices.

The New York native, aided by his father's association with John Jacob Astor, entered shipping/trading employment prior to opening his own

sugar brokerage firm. There he began his accumulation of wealth that multiplied through his association with City Bank of New York and from profits secured from iron and coal investments. Taylor had been an investor in the Delaware, Lackawanna and Western Railroad prior to his assumption of control after its stock was depressed in the Panic of 1857. Afterward, the line became an enormous profit maker. His fortune grew with other investments in real estate, communications and gas.

Taylor was not known for his generosity, but he gave a substantial sum at the end of his life for the construction of the

Moses Taylor is remembered in Long Branch by the magnificent Elberon Memorial Church.

Moses Taylor Hospital near the Scranton, Pennsylvania base of his coal operations. The nearby town of Taylor is named for him. Catherine honored him by spending a hefty sum to build the Elberon Memorial Church, located on Park Avenue, near their summer home at 1083 Ocean Avenue in the Elberon section of Long Branch. The residence was razed in 1982.

SEABURY TREDWELL (1780-1865)

Tredwell provides a link between ancient and modern Rumson. He owned an extensive estate at Black Point, formerly Passage Point, the northeastern section of the now famed suburb that formerly provided an outlet to the sea.

Born in North Hempstead, Long Island, Tredwell acquired his property in 1832–33 from a short-term owner, the equally famed Eleazar Parmly. The latter preferred a location closer to the midpoint of the Rumson–Red Bank peninsula. Tredwell's surroundings remained agrarian in his time, while maritime traffic slowed with the closing of the Sandy Hook inlet and

Seabury Tredwell's career links New York with the Jersey Shore. His Ridge Road residence was esteemed as one of the area's most historic houses until destroyed in a fire of likely incendiary origins in 2006.

the emergence of Red Bank as the leading Navesink River port. Tredwell died five years prior to the completion of the Rumson bridge to Sea Bright, a project that propelled his town's development. The breakup of his estate, which numbered two sales in his lifetime in 1847 and 1858 and many others from the 1880s, comprises a key early chapter in the making of modern Rumson. Little is known about Tredwell's life in Rumson, but his daughter Gertrude retained his little-changed house at 16 Ridge Road until 1928.

Tredwell, a New York merchant, also provides a studied link between the city and the shore. He bought his New York residence at 29 East 4th Street in 1835, a fine Greek Revival house built three years earlier. At the time, it was located on a genteel residential street that over the decades turned into a seedy commercial district. Gertrude, who over the years became an impoverished recluse, remained there until her death in 1933. Their city residence in its later incarnation as the Merchant's House Museum provides insight into nineteenth-century life in New York. The Ridge Road residence was esteemed as one of the area's most historic houses until destroyed in a fire of likely incendiary origins in 2006.

RESORTS

WILLIAM P. CHADWICK JR. (1830-?)

Chadwick is one of several Squan Beach area lodging hosts who brought their old establishments to early resort prominence without having left much of a biographical trail.

Chadwick House was founded, according to Woolman and Rose, in 1830 by James Shumard, who kept it for ten years prior to an approximate fifteen-year run by John A. Maxon, an owner succeeded by his son-in-law Chadwick. They maintained a shore presence before there was any real shore occupancy or tradition at a time when travel was long and arduous, evidenced by an 1864 account that described how the place was reached from New York "in just eight hours." Travel time eventually shortened, while their following grew after the New York and Long Branch Railroad reached Point Pleasant Beach around 1878. Located on Squan Beach about midway between Manasquan and Barnegat Inlets, the place's siting at a right angle to the beach provided unobstructed views. After expansions, Chadwick's was able to accommodate fifty around 1878.

Chadwick, who was in charge of the nearby Life Saving Station, was also engaged in wrecking, or the salvage of ships and cargo. In addition, he was held in high repute as a gunner and fisherman. Chadwick's later fell under the operation of Charles Seaman of Toms River, but it had been long closed when destroyed by fire in 1919.

JOHN CHAMBERLAIN (?–1896)

Massachusetts native Chamberlain became the forefather of Long Branch gambling after he was inspired by the belief that he could stem the summer loss of his New York business by following his customers to the Jersey Shore. His gambling house, built in the emerging Second Empire style, opened in 1868 at the southwest corner of Ocean and Brighton Avenues. Chamberlain ran a class operation, but his calling rarely attracted biographers, so a closer look requires access to the not always reliable press.

Chamberlain, who spent his early career in Missouri prior to relocating in the east in the Civil War years, probably utilized various locations over time. *Entertaining a Nation* reported on one of his at 8 West 25th Street, likely the "gambling hell in 25th Street" mentioned in an 1871 newspaper rant, while another news report indicated that Chamberlain's place at 5 West 24th Street was larger than a rival's. Chamberlain believed a racetrack would enhance the appeal of Long Branch, so in emulation of a Saratoga rival, he planned in 1869 the first Monmouth Park, which, after reorganization of his early planning group, opened the next year. Chamberlain's modus operandi was free spending and the care and feeding of those necessary to keep under his control. They included not only the law but also reporters. His fare was epicurean, while alcohol flowed freely.

A *New York Herald* writer, while reporting for an article titled "Gambling in New York" on August 19, 1870, was effusive in his description of the ten divisions of gambling in the city when he placed Chamberlain in the top class by himself. He claimed John was "as handsome a man there is in the metropolis…middle stature…compactly built with an almost perfect head, abundantly covered with fine, black silked hair…with small features." Chamberlain was never seen to frown and was one of the best natured of men.

Chamberlain sought to appeal to what are now called "high rollers." Locals were barred as he disdained the thought of taking money from workers who needed their income to support families. While Chamberlain was considered to have the consummate make-up of a gambler, the inherent risks in the field led to his insolvency in the 1870s, a forced sale to Phil Daly and Chamberlain's heading to Washington. There he replicated his gambling operation and opened the city's finest dining establishment. After he died at Saratoga, the obituary of "Jovial John Chamberlain" noted that over the past quarter-century in Washington he had been the associate of statesmen and diplomats from all over the world and had legions of friends countrywide among men of taste and wit.

RODERICK A. CLARK (1843-1929)

Before Captain Roderick A. Clark became a name on the land at Point Pleasant, good fortune and an angel of mercy brought him through a perilous experience on the Monocacy Bridge (Maryland) battlefield.

Roderick was born in Great Bend, Pennsylvania, prior to the Clark family's move to Point Pleasant after his father, John, having seen the area as a federal surveyor, believed it to be a good location for building boats. His son, who enlisted at Toms River with the Fourteenth New Jersey Volunteers in 1862, saw extensive action prior to the aforementioned fateful encounter on July 11, 1864. His unit, which had taken heavy casualties, was on the move to protect their rear line when Clark was shot in the ankle. His men were unable to remove him, especially after a second bullet that went through his lung knocked him to the ground. A third bullet narrowly missed him while he was lying there, but Clark survived to be removed to the hospital in Frederick, where need compelled citizens to enlist as volunteers. One who served was Lizzie Ott, who cared for Clark for days until his leg was amputated below the knee prior to his returning home. Clark, who recounted his Civil War memories for the *Ocean County Leader* of April 7, 1916, declared that he married her a year and a half later.

Clark built a residence and boat building business on the Manasquan River on land he bought in 1872, a tract he expanded in 1875 and 1879. As the business flourished, Clark both rented boats and attracted a growing following of picnic visitors. The two-story pavilion he built on the river in 1894 became famed as Clarks Landing. Later, he added other attractions, including dancing, movies and a photo gallery, while ice and skating activities were featured in the winter. After Clark sold the property in 1924, its subsequent decline followed a succession of owners and left only the marina, the one facility that survived 1970s residential development.

Clark was active in politics and other business pursuits. He survived both Lizzie and his second wife, the former Ida. V. Jumelle.

PHILIP DALY (C. 1835-1910)

Born in Philadelphia, Daly became Long Branch's longest-running gambling act, but early in his career, he was elected constable in Philadelphia according to the August 20, 1898 *Chicago Tribune*. As a gambling club had

Phil Daly operated the Pennsylvania Club, Long Branch's finest gambling house.

greater appeal, Daly undertook those operations in his native city, but in time, another Philadelphian, Richard J. Dobbins, attracted him to the shore.

With Dobbins's backing, Daly took over the insolvent Chamberlain operation, greatly expanded the place, renamed it the Pennsylvania Club and expanded the high-end market established by his predecessor. He built the pictured domed structures. Daly achieved his reputation by adhering to his credo of "a square deal." Trust in his integrity was implicit among his high-stakes players.

In 1888, Daly was shot by robbers in New York under mysterious circumstances. After he narrowly missed death, Daly was never the same person. Although he turned over managerial operations to his son, Phil Jr., he was described two years later as much a public character as the president. In time, especially after an ardent and successful campaign to stamp out gambling conducted by former judge and future governor John Franklin Fort, the elder Daly lived in seclusion, cared for by his devoted wife, Catherine.

Catherine's passions were incongruous with her husband's career. She not only had charitable interests, but she also had a strong, active devotion to the Roman Catholic Church. Catherine had a chapel built into their home and was a major benefactor of St. Michael's Church in West End. His seclusion led some to believe that she was a widow even prior to Phil's 1910 death.

WILLIAM ROBERT HENTGES (B. 1937)

Visitors can readily perceive that neon signs create the defining images of the Wildwoods but may not realize that the firm most responsible for the enduring signage is the ABS Sign Company, which was founded in 1963 by Bob Hentges.

Hentges began in the field employed by other firms without giving forethought of a career before going into business for himself during a boom period for Wildwood construction and signage. The completion of the Garden State Parkway to Cape May County in 1956 brought a new clientele from northern New Jersey, which transformed what had been a Philadelphia resort. During the years that followed, the replacement of faded, outdated boardinghouses by modern motels was so intense that the new owners often leaned on ABS for not only a neon sign but a name, logo and their resultant image as well. As Hentges said, "We did it all."

The neon boom faded in time. Plastic signage gained a strong foothold in the 1970s as a less-costly and more endurable alternative. The three Wildwood resorts also had their ups and downs but rebounded over time and later found appeal for second-home condominiums. Consequently, many brightly colored, idiosyncratic, perhaps funky, motels gave way to prosaic multiple dwellings.

Historians studied the Wildwood built environment of much of the second half of the twentieth century, revealed its special character that embodied a cultural trend, named the collection of eclectic modern styles "Doo-wop" with a nod to the Philadelphia pop music style and began a preservation movement. Now Doo-wop architecture not only defines the Wildwoods, but its protection is secured by ordinances. Neon was also revived in recognition that this type signage was crucial to the Wildwoods' unique quality.

Hentges's business evolved as his son Randy took over. The younger Hentges learned tube bending to keep a critical part of the operation in house. Durable neon will eventually require repair, so sign restoration became an important part of the business. Indeed, Hentges pointed out that his favorite sign project, the Cape Cod Inn, was built by him and restored by his son. Technical changes in the lights are another factor in an evolving business.

Hentges also enjoyed a career in public life, first having attained elective office in 1963 as West Wildwood's youngest mayor at age twenty-six. He won by only three votes on a ballot on which his wife was elected tax collector by ninety votes. Hentges was not concerned by his margin of victory but was gratified that many more placed their better judgment with his better half.

After his election to the office in 1972, Hentges served forty years as Cape May County surrogate.

New signs are fewer while many motels are gone, but the work of the most prolific and enduring Wildwood sign maker remains readily and brightly on view throughout the Wildwoods.

JOHN HOEY (c. 1825–1892)

John Hoey rose to renown and riches with the Adams Express Company, but a financial "embarrassment" near the end of his career cost him dearly. During his rise and peak, he built what is arguably the Jersey Shore's most lavish estate, one that embraced not only his home, but a large number of guest cottages and an extensive public garden as well. The memory of his Hollywood Park, which reflects the tract's numerous holly bushes, endures in Long Branch section and street names.

Hoey, who emigrated from Ireland as a small boy, was hired as a young man by Alvin Adams, a pioneer in the express business, a means of delivering small packages and mail and, for Adams, eventually specie for the United States Treasury, a responsibility that reflected the firm's power. Hoey left to form his own express company. His firm was later acquired by Adams, a merger that profited Hoey greatly. Hoey rose to the Adams presidency and a generous income, which he needed, as his showplace on the shore proved a money pit.

In 1862, Hoey made his first 48.5-acre purchase in the West End section. After constructing his summer home, he attracted many visitors so he built a number of guest cottages, some for rental, along with conservatories to support his ambitious horticultural pursuits. Among the artfully designed gardens were some planted to resemble Oriental carpets. The still-growing number of visitors then prompted Hoey to build the Hollywood Hotel.

Hoey took personal interest in each aspect of Hollywood Park. It was said that he designed the rental houses, known as cottages, while his oversight of garden operations in work clothes often left him indistinguishable from his grounds crew. It was reported that he shrewdly bought farm land at modest prices only to sell it reluctantly, albeit at considerably higher prices, to raise funds needed to support construction and operations. He was heavily leveraged. In 1891, after accusations of financial irregularities, Hoey was forced out of Adams, a case beyond the ambit of this profile. He died the next year, survived by his wife, the actress Josephine Hoey Shaw (see page 32) and their children.

John Hoey's gardens in his magnificent Hollywood estate included flower beds designed as Oriental carpets.

WILLIAM C. HUNT (1872-1970)

Hunt's long career in the world of entertainment brought him from a motion picture pioneer to an operator in the modern amusement park world. Born in Port Jefferson, Long Island, to a shipbuilder father, Hunt, who spent his early career in Bridgeport, Connecticut, worked in the novelty advertisement field prior to entering the entertainment business. He brought movies to Wildwood in 1906 and then in 1910 organized the United Theatre Company of Holly Beach, a firm that embraced drama and vaudeville in addition to film. By the mid-'30s, Hunt had nineteen theatres in New Jersey and Pennsylvania, along with bowling alleys and ballrooms. The latter responded to the Great Depression by sponsoring marathon dances, although his theatres also hosted welfare employment fundraisers.

Hunt, active in politics that decade, served three years in the New Jersey State Assembly, although the refusal of Judge Wilfred Jayne to certify his election to the state senate over fraud issues prompted Hunt to leave the upper house.

After Hunt bought the failing Ocean Pier in 1935, which had devolved to the site of a ballroom, he added rides and maintained the repurposed pier until its destruction by fire on December 25, 1943. Reconstruction would take some years, due not only to wartime materials scarcity but also to await the rebound of the county's resort industry. When a rebuilt pier devoted to rides opened in June 1957, the year after the Garden State Parkway reached Cape May County, *Billboard* remarked on June 10, 1957, that it "will help fill the amusement void created when State law closed down the bumper crop of games that represented a major amusement at this South Jersey resort." *Billboard* alluded to the legal campaign to clean up games of chance that were characterized as gambling. The Flyer, a wood roller coaster, was a major draw. The next year, the addition of the Jungleland boat ride proved enormously popular. Hunt's Pier would become a legend.

Hunt helped revitalize the Wildwood Golf Club in 1921 and revive the Cape May County Chamber of Commerce after the war, an organization he served for a spell as president. He was also president of the Wildwood Trust Company and publisher of the *Wildwood Leader*. His amusement pier came to an end with its purchase by the Morey organization in 1999.

Charles H. Jenkinson (?-1937)

When Charles H. Jenkinson made his January 1926 purchase of beachfront property from Augustus C. Hayes, as recorded in Book 680 of Ocean Deeds, page 200, he did not imagine that this was the beginning of what would become virtually a second name for the Ocean County summer resort town. Two years later, he started what became today's Jenkinson's Boardwalk.

Little is known of the apparent one-time railroad worker who, upon seeing the appeal of the Asbury Park–Ocean Grove area, decided to open rented refreshment concessions. His boardwalk operation began in 1928 with his usual food and drink stand, an open-air beach pavilion and a novelty store, as well as a saltwater swimming pool filled with filtered seawater. A dance floor and miniature golf course followed the next year, while the pavilion was enlarged and enclosed. Incremental improvements that followed over the years continued after the founder's 1937 death and succession by his son Orlo.

Ownership of the boardwalk and beachfront has had a checkered history in Point Pleasant Beach. The borough eschewed ownership of the waterfront in 1897 for reasons of cost. As late as 1911 and perhaps afterward, the privately owned boardwalk was rolled up each winter. A town improvement association sparked the initiative for much work that decade, which included a permanent boardwalk in 1915. Jenkinson's foresight enabled

The Jenkinsons owned the beach, which enabled them to run a once popular miniature railroad there.

the firm to acquire most of the oceanfront and the income from beach fees, a factor that still impacts the town, which has an excessive dependency on parking fees and fines for income. Jenkinson was also able in 1949 to install on the beach one of their most appealing features, a miniature railroad that operated until 1996. The business passed from family hands in 1977.

While the area over the years endured battering by storms, wartime restrictions and the ravages of fire, change was a constant. The greatest was the June 1991 opening of Jenkinson's Aquarium. The generations passed, the family moved on, but Charles's modest beginnings are fixed as the Jenkinson Boardwalk.

Wilbert C. Morey (1927–1998)

The Morey brothers were fundamental to the 1950s rebirth of the Wildwoods. From early beginnings with motels, they built an entertainment empire. Will was the cornerstone of the building operation.

The West Wildwood native learned construction from his father, a carpenter with the Coast Guard. An outlandish 1956 motel, the Fantasy, signaled a revolutionary new era for Wildwood lodging in a resort that was newly emerging from Cape May County's post–World War II slumber. Its flamboyant architectural features and its bright, flashing, super-sized neon sign commanded attention. The Fantasy became symbolic of the new Wildwood. Will went on to own nearly thirty motels of trendsetting design. The Fantasy, razed in 2005, was a loss during an era when a new trend emerged in the Wildwoods, the replacement of old motels, many of them family owned, by condominiums. The Fantasy is considered the first of what became known as Doo-wop motels, a building group now protected by preservation ordinances (see page 125).

The amusement end of the operation would expand to greater heights, spearheaded by Will's brother William, or Bill, who had earlier focused on boardwalk concessions. After the two observed in Florida during the fall of 1968 a twelve-lane fiberglass slide, they installed a similar one the next season in Wildwood. Called the Wipe-Out, this major success was the start of a growing passion for amusements. Morey features, which expanded incrementally, included the Zipper and miniature golf in 1970, while the King Kong airplane ride followed in 1971. They bought the Marine Pier in 1976 and then renamed it Mariner's Landing.

The brothers' travels took them to Germany to keep on top of an evolving industry. Their greatest success is arguably the roller coasters, first the Great Nor'easter in 1995, followed by the even greater Great White in 1996, which was the first modern wood roller coaster erected in the Wildwoods since 1919. This 3,300-foot-long ride brought great media attention at its debut.

At publication, the Morey Organization, dominant in Wildwood amusements, can trace its beginnings to the now historic motels built by Will Morey.

William Sandlass (1862–1938)

The observer may not readily determine where the recreational area of the Jersey Shore began, as Sandy Hook has been entirely a federal reservation for two centuries. The now desolate area around the Highlands–Sea Bright (Captain Joseph A. Azzolina Memorial) Bridge provides little hint, but for over a half-century, William Sandlass operated a major excursion resort there.

Born in Shrewsbury, Pennsylvania, Sandlass learned carpentry from his woodworker father before he relocated to New York, where he engaged in alcoholic beverage sales. Around 1889, Sandlass arrived at the Jersey Shore to oversee the recreational component of Highland Beach, a summer housing venture at the northern reach of the privately owned section of the barrier island that was then part of Ocean Township and named for the local railroad station. He appears to have been the lessee of Ferdinand Fish, a real estate promoter with a penchant for finding himself at odds with his sponsors and associates. After Fish departed to the nearby mainland to develop Water Witch Park, now Monmouth Hills, Sandlass became an owner. His Sandlass Pavilion, also known as Highland Beach, was an excursion resort, a type of facility that accommodated day-trippers. Sandlass regularly made improvements. His gravity railroad, a forerunner of the roller coaster, was a popular feature. The Sandlass Bamboo Garden, which was made from bamboo brought back from a 1908 trip to Jamaica, became a major draw. That trip took the life of Bill's first wife, who became ill at sea and died in a New York hospital two weeks after their return.

Sandlass prospered at Highland Beach, but presumably his wealth also came from New York ventures. He was well off in 1912 when the press recounted Bill's courtship of his second wife, Helen. The fifty-year-old spent two years wooing the "telephone girl" at the Hotel Gerard in midtown New York before she agreed to wed this man twice her age. Their courtship appealed to the contemporary press such as the September 29, 1912 *Miami Herald*, which repeated the item from the *New York World*.

Sandlass engaged in other local business activities, as the Pavilion was seasonal. Operations at the amusement park came to a standstill as World War II choked travel access. The resort evolved over time to a beach club. Eventually the buildings disappeared as the federal government took the property located at the doorstep of a critical military base, one that is now a major National Park Service recreational area. All that remains is the former Sandlass residence, which at publication is threatened with destruction.

HENRY WASHINGTON SAWYER (1830–1893)

Captain Sawyer built a career as a Cape May hotel operator following considerable notoriety as a condemned Civil War prisoner. Obviously, he had been spared.

Sawyer, born in Lehigh County, Pennsylvania, trained as a carpenter after arriving in Cape May in 1848. After he enlisted early in the war as a private, Sawyer received a commission and then rose in rank. Wounded at the great cavalry battle at Brandy Station, Virginia, in June 1863, he was captured and sent to Libby Prison, Richmond, where he was one of two captains' names chosen by lot to be executed in retaliation for the Union's execution of two Confederate captains who were captured while recruiting in Union territory. His heartfelt letter from prison to his wife, which has been quoted often, includes: "My dear wife, the fortune of war has put me in this position. If I must die a sacrifice to my country, with God's will I must submit; only let me see you once more, and I will die becoming a man and an officer."

After vigorous Union protestations delayed the planned execution, he languished at Libby until exchanged in March 1864.

Sawyer became proprietor of the Ocean House in 1867, staying until he left to open the Clayton House in Wilmington, Delaware. He remained there for two and a half years, prior to his return to Cape May to build the Chalfonte Hotel, which he operated until his death. Sawyer was elected for several terms to the city council and served as a superintendent of the Life Saving Service.

Captain Clarence W. Starn (1890-1969)

After Captain Starn opened the second of Atlantic City's two large seafood restaurants, he built his inlet operation into an entertainment center. He is fondly remembered by an aging former clientele, as are his passenger-carrying sailboats that provided legions with ocean-bound views of the shore.

Born in Cumberland County, Clarence moved to Atlantic City as a youth. In the World War I years, he obtained a master's license and served as an officer on cross-Atlantic steamships. After the war, he had a bi-state boating business here and in Miami. Following the loss of his vessel in a 1928 Florida hurricane, Starn briefly became a strawberry farmer in Florida. He returned to New Jersey and bought a boat financed by Harry Hackney, which he used to promote the latter's massive seafood establishment. Starn's Seafood Restaurant opened at his Inlet Pier located northwest of the boardwalk in 1940 near Hackney's. He frequently expanded the facility with the expectation that its features and exhibitions would make the place a recreation destination in its own right. The bar in the rear attracted well-dressed convention-goers who after dinner mingled with the fisher folks. A clam bar provided informal eating, and following the 1944 hurricane, a "Captain's Bridge" dining room was fashioned from a yacht after its stern was removed. An upstairs dining room followed in the late 1940s, and a "Captain's Mess," originally for early-bird breakfast service, was kept open for informal dining. Starn also maintained a gift shop, ice cream stand, wishing well and duck pond. A more ambitious operation was a photography studio that processed a variety of souvenir images. At various times, Starn included a funhouse, fortuneteller and pony rides. The maritime world offered an aquarium, bait and tackle stand, rental boats and exhibition fish, including one large, dead shark that was shown while placed on ice for preservation. They collected a dime for each admission until the smell became overwhelming. Visitors bought small pieces of fish for the fun of feeding the sea lions. Porpoises were displayed around 1960, but because they could not be convinced to leave the premises for the south in the winter, they had the misfortune to die here.

The inlet declined with Atlantic City's slow, steady fall from grace, which later accelerated and had become glaring by the 1970s. Starn's closed in 1979.

JOSIAH H. WHITE III (c. 1840-1914)

Atlantic City's generational change in its hotel stock is determined more by building substance than by time, but the process can be traced back for well over a century. The leadership of Josiah H. White III was crucial during two key periods.

Our subject, the son of prominent Philadelphia Quaker minister John Josiah, was named for an uncle. He farmed in his earlier years, first in Pemberton, Burlington County, and then on Maryland's eastern shore, prior to opening a canning factory there. Returning in 1888 to Philadelphia and the New Jersey roots of ancient family ties, White purchased Atlantic City's Luray boardinghouse and enlarged it four years later prior to building a new Luray in 1895. The place on the boardwalk, which featured hot and cold seawater baths, was destroyed in the great Atlantic City conflagration of April 3, 1902. The boom in business that year and the critical need for accommodations prompted the mayor to ask residents to rent spare rooms.

That year, White began the construction of William L. Price's (see page 21) design for the Marlborough Hotel, which established a new standard for modernity and comfort. They teamed to expand in 1905–06 with the separate Blenheim, which White soon linked with the Marlborough as a single operation. The Blenheim's tower, constructed of reinforced concrete, a relatively new building material that addressed the city's emerging fire protection standards, was the largest such structure in the world. The owner-architect team later combined for the

Josiah White regularly improved Atlantic City's hotel stock. The Traymore was his last great project.

Traymore, which set new standards for luxury and reinforced concrete, but its 1915 completion followed the owner's death. Two of his sons, John Josiah and Charles, were appointed to the bench, while a third, Allen, was a mechanical engineer, who remained active with the firm Josiah White & Son, Company.

CAPTAIN JOHN L. YOUNG (1853–?)

Captain Young rose from a modest beginning to become a master showman. He took waterfront entertainment to new heights and even new depths, as Young made the daily unloading of deep-sea fishing vessels a tourist attraction.

Born in Absecon to an oysterman father, Young, who became a lifeguard at Atlantic City at age twenty, began work as a fisherman. After he took up carpentry, Young built a number of houses and then Young's Hotel. He reportedly made a tidy sum by investing in a beachfront tract that was sold

Captain John Young garnered much publicity by giving his house the address "1 Atlantic Ocean."

by a wary owner who was distressed over damage by a recent storm and fearful of additional damage. In time, Young reportedly owned about ten miles by the beachfront. "Captain" was an honorific given him through winter service on the police force.

Young purchased Applegate's Pier with a partner, which he extended to two thousand feet and then renamed for himself. He enhanced its appeal by adding attractions, which included a roller-skating rink and theatre. Following the sale of Young's Pier in 1905, Young, in conjunction with Philadelphia contractor Kennedy Crosson, built the Young Million Dollar Pier the next year. The immediate success of the new Young's Pier established a new standard for oceanfront entertainment.

Young's fanciful house, essentially an Italianate design, perhaps more fittingly called "Italian wedding cake style," was built at the foot of Arkansas Avenue adjacent to his pier. Its decoration reflected the captain's preference for the fanciful and maritime themes. He also owned a number of hotels, land in Florida and a number of watercraft.

SPIRITUAL

Reverend Michael L. Glennon (1852-1900)

While the first assignment of Michael Glennon was in Jersey City, Hudson County, a cornerstone in the establishment of Roman Catholicism in New Jersey, he spent little time ministering to the immigrants so important to the expansion of the church. Father Glennon was sent to the Jersey Shore, where he became a builder of churches.

After Michael Lynch Glennon, born to a farming family at Crohan, County Cavan, Ireland, emigrated to New York in 1870, he studied at the Seminary of the Holy Angels, Niagara Falls, and the Seminary at Seton Hall, South Orange, New Jersey. Following ordination in 1877, Glennon was sent to St. Bridget's, Jersey City, but he remained only about a year and a half. While there, he wrote a catechism that won wide acceptance in New Jersey and elsewhere prior to its mandatory replacement in 1884 by the Baltimore Catechism. He was then assigned to build a church at Everett, on the Holmdel-Middletown border. After completing St. Catharine of Genoa, Glennon was assigned as pastor in Asbury Park. After Father Glennon built that city's Holy Spirit, St. Catharine became its mission church. Father Glennon's next assignments were to build churches at Lakehurst, then Belmar (now St. Rose), followed by St. Ann's (as the name was then spelled) in Spring Lake, a parish renamed St. Catharine after the present magnificent edifice was completed in 1903 (see page 111).

Reverend Michael Glennon was the priest who built churches.

While the New Jersey church was becoming well established in the growing cities, the Catholic population in the rural areas was often sparse, which required Father Glennon to travel each Sunday to minister to multiple congregations. His congenial personality and diplomatic skills greatly aided the growth of Catholicity on the shore. He was beloved by his people, respected by a wide circle and served as a welcoming host to many visiting clergy. His zeal and eagerness to reach as many as possible led to overwork.

Father Glennon suffered from pneumonia in the winter of 1896 and then malarial fever during a trip to the South. Having earlier traveled abroad, he made what he hoped would be a convalescing trip to Ireland in September 1900. He died in Killarney on October 15. After his body was returned the next spring, there followed extensive expressions of mourning and interment at Mount Calvary Cemetery near the Asbury Park and ocean that he loved.

REVEREND ELLWOOD HAINES STOKES (1815–1897)

Stokes, born on a Medford, Burlington County farm to a Quaker family, was apprenticed as a youth to a Philadelphia bookbinder prior to studying for the ministry. After licensure by the Methodist Episcopal Church around 1842, he served in various four-year assignments throughout New Jersey

Dr. Stokes claimed to be an originator of the Methodist summer camp custom, both rural, such as Pitman, New Jersey, and seashore, notably Ocean Grove. His extensive writings include a historical sketch of the founding of

Reverend Ellwood Stokes was the key figure in the creation of
Ocean Grove.

Ocean Grove. The place was initially planned as a small retreat on the six
acres purchased on carefully chosen grounds at a locale about six miles south
of the well-known Long Branch resort. The large following they attracted
resulted that winter in the organization of the Ocean Grove Camp Meeting
Association of the Methodist Episcopal Church. The group succeeded in a
campaign to acquire land that totaled 230 acres by 1872 and to build streets
on rough property recently overgrown or barren.

Dr. Stokes, the longtime corresponding editor of the *Ocean Grove Record*,
wrote two books of verse, *Blossoms* and *Starlets by the Sea*, a volume on his

foreign travels, as well as the *Annual Reports of the Association* from 1870 to 1896. Dr. Stokes, who was the first president of the association, served many years in that office and planned the Grove's greatest landmark, the Great Auditorium, built in 1894. He is considered "the father of Ocean Grove."

The statue, funded by public subscription and sculpted by Paul W. Morris of New York, was unveiled on July 31, 1905, on Ocean Grove's Memorial Day. This was the occasion for honoring friends of the Grove who passed in the prior year and the thirty-fifth anniversary of the Grove. Stokes's career and dedication were lauded by Bishop Henry Spellmerer and Governor Edward C. Stokes, a distant relative. It faces the ocean on Pilgrim Pathway with the Great Auditorium at its rear.

SPORTS

Frank Budd (1939-2014)

Budd once held the honorific of the "world's fastest human." The exploits that reached that pinnacle began at Asbury Park High School in the city where, later in life, Budd would be honored as one of New Jersey's all-time great athletes.

Budd was a high school standout in football, basketball and track. After Frank focused on the latter following the acceptance of a scholarship to Villanova, he became one of the world's outstanding sprinters. He participated in two events in the 1960 Olympics in Rome. Although the American team finished first in the four-hundred-meter relay, they missed the gold medal due to disqualification resulting from a faulty baton pass. Budd's greatest achievement was attained the following year when he broke the world record for the one-hundred-yard dash. He returned to football in order to earn a living from his athleticism, and despite not having played in college, he was drafted by the Philadelphia Eagles. He played briefly for them as a receiver and then later with the Washington Redskins prior to two years with Calgary in the Canadian Football League.

Budd resided in Mount Laurel later in life but returned to Asbury Park for honors bestowed including the Frank Budd Track Meet on the Frank Budd Oval at the high school stadium and, in 2007, the Shore Athletic Club's Frank Budd Recognition and Scholarship Fund Dinner. He was one of the first class of athletes honored on the Villanova Wall of Fame.

ROGER MAXWELL "DOC" CRAMER (1905-1990)

If the baseball axiom that home run hitters get the glory while singles hitters get overlooked is true, then Doc Cramer provides vivid evidence from Ocean County. Impressive numbers during a twenty-year major league career have fallen short of the ultimate honor, enshrinement in the Hall of Fame.

Born in Beach Haven, Cramer moved as a young boy to Manahawkin. He acquired his lifelong nickname through friendship with local physician Joshua Hilliard, whom he often accompanied on his local rounds. During a tryout, after Cramer impressed legendary Philadelphia Athletics owner-manager Connie Mack, he was signed to a contract and then brought along slowly. He reached the major leagues for two games in 1929, the first of his long career with four teams. After Cramer became an every-day player, he led the league in at bats three consecutive years and became a .300 hitter but was traded in 1936 to the Boston Red Sox. Boston became his favorite team. Cramer was selected an All-Star in the last four of the five seasons he spent with them, prior to going to the Washington Senators in 1941. He was a regular with the Detroit Tigers during the four war years, which included their 1945 World Series win over the Chicago Cubs. Relegated to part-time play in 1946, Cramer ended his career with four games in 1948.

Doc Cramer's supporters wonder how he is denied admission to the Hall of Fame despite an outstanding career. *Courtesy of Ocean County Historical Society.*

Cramer's fine statistics include 2,705 hits, while as a centerfielder, he ranks third all-time in games played at that crucial position. He had eight .300 seasons, led the league in hits in 1940 and in pinch-hits in 1947, while he twice accomplished the rare feat of six hits in six bats. Cramer, who was a carpenter in his later years, built his own home in Manahawkin, where he was a member of the Masons and the Stafford Township Volunteer Fire Department.

Local advocacy for Cramer's admission to the Hall has been ardent, albeit unsuccessful, prompting speculation on why not. His statistics are very good, but not great. If a lack of power fails to garner respect, so do seasons played during the depleted World War II years. Cramer never led the league in batting, while his lifetime .296 average and 2,705 hits fall short of the traditional .300 and 3,000 benchmarks. Many have attained 2,700 hits in recent decades without strong Hall candidacy. Luck or a friend on the old-timers selection committee can help, suggested by others with less impressive credentials having been chosen. Whether or not Cramer will be honored in Cooperstown, he is recognized in Manahawkin by Doc Cramer Boulevard.

CLEVELAND GAITER (1906–1944)

Cleveland Gaiter's story may have remained obscure had not Gil Leibrick begun research that he shared with me to find worthy old-timer candidates for the Toms River High School's Athletic Hall of Fame. Gaiter's extraordinary accomplishments earned him stature as arguably the system's greatest all-time athlete. He had to overcome obstacles that included racism and a lack of equal opportunity.

Wilfred and Ernestine Gaiter, immigrants from the Bahamas, settled in Seaside Heights sometime in the early twentieth century, where they were among few other black residents. He was employed, and they ran a small hotel for African Americans. The place was reportedly an after-hours relaxation venue for performers of all races. Their ten children went to Toms River High School, beginning with daughter Olive. There, Cleveland became a standout in three sports, including track and field and baseball, but his greatest exploits were on the gridiron.

Gaiter, whose career spanned 1923–25, had an outstanding senior year during which he led the then small school, which competed with larger schools, to a second-place statewide rank. His outstanding performance earned him second team all-state honors, a rare accomplishment for a player from the then often-overlooked Ocean County. His junior year was marred by a racial incident in which Point Pleasant High School players attempted to remove him from the game by deliberate injury, an ugly event abetted by local game officials.

In the spring, Gaiter played in the outfield and pitched. Gaiter displayed enormous stamina in track competitions, as he ran both sprints and a relay, put the shot and participated in both the high and broad jumps. He typically either won or placed among the top finishers. Following high school, Gaiter played semiprofessional football and undertook a boxing career that was cut short by injury. He later became a local entertainer.

The solid accomplishments of his siblings are part of the Gaiter family legacy. Seven became teachers; two served in World War II. Roger, a pilot with the Tuskegee Airmen, was shot down on his fifty-sixth mission. After a spell as a prisoner of war, he was discharged with an elevation of rank to captain. Worrell earned a Bronze Star during the Battle of the Bulge. Cleveland was a candidate for higher education, but the eldest son in a laboring environment was expected to work. His son Roger told of their discovering many years later a letter from Columbia that offered a full scholarship. While opportunity was lost, Cleveland's career merits celebration and a place in history.

AL LEITER (B. 1965)

Perhaps no pitcher enjoyed a more spectacular prelude to a long major league career than Alois Terry Leiter's senior year at Central Regional High School. Following his playing days, Leiter made a fine transition to broadcaster and charitable activist.

Born in Toms River and raised in Bayville, in 1984, Leiter pitched four no-hitters and struck out thirty-two batters in a single game. It was a thirteen-inning 0–0 tie that is legendary in shore high school annals. Leiter set nearly every Central Regional pitching record and then was picked in the second round of the draft by the New York Yankees.

Leiter joined the Yankees in 1987, winning his debut appearance at age twenty-one. He pitched nineteen years in the majors with four teams, compiling a 162-132 won-lost record along with an earned-run average of 3.80. His greatest success was in 1998 with the New York Mets, when he went 17-6 with a 2.47 ERA. In 1996, while with the Florida Marlins, Leiter led the National League with the lowest batting average against. This was also the year he pitched a no-hitter. After world championship seasons in

1993 and 1997 with the Toronto Blue Jays and Marlins respectively, Leiter completed his career in 2005 with a second stint with the Yankees.

Leiter is now a thoughtful television analyst and active in charitable work. He created and leads Leiter's Landing, an organization that seeks betterment in the lives of its selected youth. Leiter's outstanding shore career earned him selection on the *Star-Ledger's* New Jersey High School Baseball Team of the Century.

WRITERS

KATHERINE BAKER (1882?–1919)

Katherine Baker's singular path to the Jersey Shore embraced work as both lawyer and fiction writer, which may make her difficult to categorize. However, her recognition stems from renown as a war heroine.

Baker, the first female admitted to the bar in Union County, Pennsylvania, practiced law in Lewisburg with her father, J. Thompson Baker (see page 41). A talented writer, her stories were published in magazines and literary journals.

Prior to the American entry into the Great War, Baker left for Paris on March 10, 1917, to join her sister Frances. She intended to stay only a short while. Following two and a half months training at the Red Cross School at Paris, she was sent to a field hospital, where three weeks later she was appointed head night nurse. After Baker became attached to the 137th Regiment and promoted to corporal, she became so absorbed in her work that she remained for two years. While at the front, she reportedly wrote magazine articles and used those earnings to buy delicacies for troops in her care. Baker contracted pneumonia, attributed to a physical breakdown caused by overwork, a condition that prompted her return to the United States and travel to a Saranac Lake sanitarium for treatment. In September, the children of Wildwood presented Baker with a medal of appreciation. Her vitality spent, Baker weakened and died on September 23, 1919.

France awarded Baker the Croix de Guerre and a Fourragere. Ten years later, the Women's Overseas Service Convention designated her one of the four outstanding heroines of the Great War. Baker was buried in Saranac Lake. When her father died several weeks later, his passing was attributed to a broken heart.

STEPHEN CRANE (1871-1900)

Stephen Crane's Jersey Shore experience was neither happy nor successful, but the journalistic beginnings of his celebrated literary career were propelled here. His Asbury Park home, the only surviving residence associated with Crane, merits preservation as a literary landmark.

Born in Newark to a Methodist minister and a Women's Christian Temperance Union–activist mother, the family moved in 1882, two years after his father died, to Arbutus Cottage at 508 Fourth Avenue. His mother, Helen Peck Crane, sought to be close to the Ocean Grove base of her operations, work that preoccupied her. Thus, Stephen was virtually raised by his elder sister Agnes. Crane lacked scholarly inclination, so after he later moved to New York, Crane found it easy to fall into the underside of city life and develop the bad habits that contributed to his ruin—heavy smoking and poor nutrition. His brother Townley, who edited the Asbury Park *Shore Press* and served as area correspondent for the *New York Tribune* and the Associated Press, assigned Stephen local stories. Crane's disdain for the place emerged in his writing. He claimed, "Asbury Park creates nothing. It does not make; it merely amuses...This is a resort of wealth and leisure, of women and considerable wine." Crane's observations were called "satirical" but were at times cynical, such as his well-known 1892 reportage of a parade of the Junior Order of United American Mechanics. This piece, although intended as barbs against the rich, was interpreted as an attack on the workingman, which resulted in both Cranes losing their positions. Stephen wrote on other shore subjects, but he had a penchant for crafting accounts without his actual physical presence.

After Crane returned to New York, he self-published the first of his two fiction masterpieces, *Maggie—A Girl of the Streets*, but was discouraged by its dismal sales. In 1895, Crane, desperate for money, agreed to serial publication of the second, *The Red Badge of Courage*. This account of a battle-seared Civil War soldier cemented his reputation.

Later, Crane and a Florida madam, Cora Taylor, passed as husband and wife, although not actually married. They traveled while he sought the war action as a correspondent that he had described without having experienced. In 1899, when the pair lived in the ruins of a fourteenth-century English manor, Crane associated with famous writers including Henry James, Ford Madox Ford and Joseph Conrad. He died of tuberculosis the next year while in a German spa.

Writing about Crane in-depth poses challenges, as he kept no journals. In addition, few letters and only one notebook survive. He has, however, reached the pinnacle of critical acclaim despite his inauspicious beginnings at the Jersey Shore.

RICHARD HARDING DAVIS (1864–1916)

Although Davis was one of the best-known writers of his time, memory of him has faded; he is all but forgotten by recent generations. Davis, however, never forgot pleasurable memories of his early days at Point Pleasant.

Davis was born in Philadelphia to a family of writers. His father, L. Clark Davis, was editor of the *Public Ledger* (see George W. Childs, page 107) while his mother, who held title to the Point Pleasant house since about 1880, was also a writer. His brother, the theatrical producer Charles Belmont Davis, crafted short stories and a memoir of his brother, *Adventures and Letters of Richard Harding Davis*. Published the year after the subject's death, the book depicts the Davis youths' fond recollections of the Jersey Shore:

> *Point Pleasant itself was then a collection of half a dozen big farms, which stretched from the Manasquan River to the ocean, half a mile distant. Nothing could have been more primitive or as I remember it in the pastoral loveliness or much more beautiful. Just beyond our cottage the river ran its silent, lazy course to the sea. With the exception of several farm houses, its banks were unsullied by human habitation of any sort, and on either side beyond the low green banks lay fields of wheat and corn and dense groves of pine and oak and chestnut trees.*

Following his first and best novel, *Soldiers of Fortune*, in 1897, the prolific Davis published nearly a book a year. After journalistic beginnings with local newspapers, he traveled the world as a reporter. Davis's fame as a leading

Richard Harding Davis's good, rugged masculine visage is believed to have made him the model for Charles Dana Gibson's "Gibson Man."

war correspondent began with reportage from Cuba during the Spanish-American War. His subsequent war coverage emerged from the Boer War in South Africa, the Greco-Turkish War in the Balkans, the Russo-Japanese War, Latin American revolutions and the Great War. The latter experience very well may have led to his premature death.

This adventure-seeking sensationalist was a premier practitioner of the era's yellow journalism. Admittedly, pandering in this style led to his stature as the best-known journalist of the day. Davis's good, rugged masculine visage is believed to have made him the model for Charles Dana Gibson's "Gibson Man."

DOROTHY PARKER (1893-1967)

Dorothy Parker actually has an accidental tie to the Jersey Shore, but she and her Long Branch birth site are celebrated on the Friends of Libraries USA Literary Landmarks Register. She was a quintessential New Yorker who over her entire life regretted her New Jersey nativity, an "accident" that resulted from her arrival in August. Then her parents were resident in the Henry Rothschild 732 Ocean Avenue, West End summer home. Parker is one of America's celebrated female writers of her generation.

Parker was closely identified with the Algonquin Round Table, a gathering of the sharp, clever and witty who met at New York's hotel of that name. She specialized in criticism, verse and the short story, but Parker was known

Dorothy Parker loved dogs and martinis, so she can be forgiven her caustic pen and disdain for New Jersey.

for her satirical, biting humor that regularly crossed the line of caustic. She held prominent positions at *Vanity Fair* and the *New Yorker*. While she became established under her maiden name prior to a 1917 marriage to Edwin Pond Parker II, she retained his name after their 1922 separation and eventual divorce. Although her life at that time took a turn to depression and alcoholism, the 1920s saw much of her best work. After she married her second husband in 1934, a younger actor named Alan Campbell, they left for Hollywood to pursue screenwriting, a move that diminished her output.

Parker's two great loves were her dogs and martinis. Her devotion to her canine companions had to be noticed, as she took them everywhere, regardless of "no animal" constraints. Many have a favorite Parker aphorism or quote. The martini lover may be partial to: "I'd like to have a martini/Two at the very most/At three I'm under the table/At four I'm under the host."

Parker died in 1967 with no known survivors. She left her modest estate, including copyrights, to Martin Luther King, with the instruction it be conveyed to the National Association for the Advancement of Colored People. Parker was not known to have been active in civil rights matters in later life, but she had long been an advocate of liberal causes. Recent years have seen a revival in an interest of Parker, including the organization of a Dorothy Parker Society. She was honored with a commemorative postage stamp in the Literary Arts series; the August 22, 1992 First Day of Issue ceremonies were held in West End Park, a few hundred yards north of her birth site. A plaque marks the historical significance of the lot that is now filled with modern multiple dwellings.

ROBERT LOUIS STEVENSON (1850-1894)

Stevenson's tie to the Jersey Shore became fixed after he spent only one month in Brielle in 1888. However, it was a stay that became shrouded in legend. Stevenson had pleasurable moments there, but ill health marred his Jersey Shore experience.

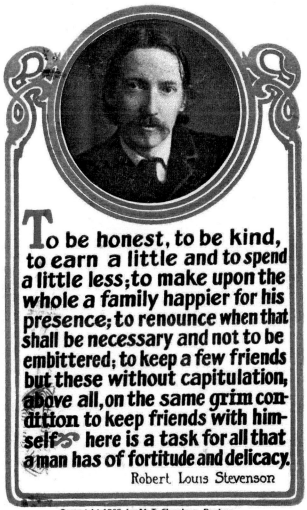

To be honest, to be kind, to earn a little and to spend a little less; to make upon the whole a family happier for his presence; to renounce when that shall be necessary and not to be embittered; to keep a few friends but these without capitulation, above all, on the same grim condition to keep friends with himself; here is a task for all that a man has of fortitude and delicacy.

Robert Louis Stevenson

Copyright 1908 by M T. Sheahan, Boston

Robert Louis Stevenson had a brief stay in Brielle, but one that firmly fixed him in shore lore. This piece may not have been written on the shore, but it is a worthy philosophy for all times and places.

After Stevenson came to the shore at the behest of his writer friend Will H. Low, he stayed at the Union House on the Manasquan River. His often-quoted letter to editor and friend Sidney Colvin waxed enthusiastic about his environs:

> *We are here at a delightful country inn, like a country French place, the only people in the house, a cat-boat at our disposal, the sea always audible on the outer beach, the lagoon as smooth as glass, all the little, queer, many coloured villas standing shuttered and empty; in front of ours, across the lagoon, two long wooden bridges, one for the rail, one for the road, sounding with intermittent traffic. It is highly pleasant, and a delightful change from Saranac. My health is much better for the change.*

After they sailed to what is now officially known as Nienstedt Island, some writers claimed the two dubbed the spot "Treasure Island" after Stevenson's novel of five years earlier. Fabricated legend even claims the local stay inspired that work, although the book was already in print. The island in the Manasquan has been known informally as Treasure Island for many decades.

His health was still questionable at best. Twenty years later, it was recalled in the November 26, 1909 *New Jersey Courier* that "Stevenson in those [days] at Brielle that he even then did his writing sitting up in bed, so weak was he from consumption, and that he invariably wore a dressing gown of red flannel, in an apparent attempt to disguise even to himself the frequency of the hemorrhages to which he was subject." Stevenson completed his plans to sail for the South Seas while in Brielle. He spent his final productive years on an island in the Samoas, never returning to his native land.

SELECTED BIBLIOGRAPHY

Barber, John W., and Henry Howe. *Historical Collections of the State of New Jersey*. New York: S. Tuttle, 1845.

Colrick, Patricia F. *A Centennial History of Saint Catharine Church*. Franklin, TN: Providence House Publishers, 2001.

Colvin, Sidney, ed. *The Letters of Robert Louis Stevenson*. Vol. 3. New York: Charles Scribner's Sons, 1911.

Francis, David W., et al. *Wildwood-by-the-Sea: The History of an American Resort*. Fairview Park, OH: Amusement Park Books, Inc., 1998.

Gabrielan, Randall. *Long Branch—Reinventing a Resort*. Atglen, PA: Schiffer Publishers, 2009.

Jahn, Robert. *Down Barnegat Bay—A Nor'easter Reader*. Mantoloking, NJ: Beachcomber Press, 1980.

Johnson, Nelson. *Boardwalk Empire*. Medford, NJ: Plexus Publishing, 2002.

McCarter, G.W.C. "The Proprietor." Forthcoming biography of George W. Childs.

Nelson, William. *The New Jersey Coast in Three Centuries*. New York: Lewis Historical Publishing Co., 1902.

Pederson, Roy. *Jersey Shore Impressionists—The Fascination of Sun and Sea*. West Creek, NJ: Down the Shore Publishing, 2013.

Rose, T.F. *Historical and Biographical Atlas of the New Jersey Coast*. Philadelphia, PA: 1878. (Known as Woolman and Rose)

Schnitzspahn, Karen L. *Stars of the New Jersey Shore—A Theatrical History*. Atglen, PA: Schiffer Publishers, 2007.

SELECTED BIBLIOGRAPHY

Stellhorn, Paul A., and Michael J. Birkner. *The Governors of New Jersey, 1664–1974, Biographical Essays*. Trenton, NJ: New Jersey Historical Commission, 1982.

Wilson, Harold F. *The Jersey Shore*. 3 vols. New York: Lewis Historical Publishing Co., 1953.

NEWSPAPERS, MANY, NOTABLY

New Jersey Courier
New York Times
Philadelphia Inquirer
Red Bank Register

INDEX

INDEX

INDEX

INDEX

ABOUT THE AUTHOR

Native New Jerseyan Randall Gabrielan is a member of the Monmouth County Historical Commission, having recently retired as its long-term executive director, and the county's officially appointed historian. He has written and lectured extensively on a variety of New Jersey subjects along the shore and elsewhere, as well as having written on New York, where he worked for a prolonged spell, and Brooklyn, where he resided for ten years.

The author is pictured at the Naval Air Station Wildwood Museum standing beside a MiG-15. *Photograph by Robert Pellegrini.*

Visit us at
www.historypress.net

....

This title is also available as an e-book